BIENVENIDOS

(Bilingual/Bicultural Teacher's Resource Guide To Mexico)

by
Cynthia Downs & Terry Becker

illustrated by
Margherita DePaulis

Publishers
T.S. Denison and Company, Inc.
Minneapolis, Minnesota 55431

Standard Book Number: 513-02053-5
Bienvenidos
Copyright © 1991 by T.S. Denison & Co., Inc.
Minneapolis, Minnesota 55431

Introduction

Dear Readers,

¡Bienvenidos! ¡Vámonos (o) venga con nosotros a México!

Welcome! Come with us to Mexico!

The purpose of this book is not to give you, the teacher, a day by day lesson plan but it is to acquaint you with the language and customs of Mexico. Also, it is our desire to share with you a part of Mexico's rich culture and heritage and to help you incorporate this culture into the daily classroom routine.

It would take an encyclopedia to effectively include all the language, culture, history, music, art, etc. and etc. Therefore, we have tried to include a variety of information and activities so that you will be able to enrich the child's knowledge of his/her "neighbor to the south."

The material is organized into twelve different chapters for you to do with as you wish. The chapters are broken down into months of the year that would correspond with other curriculum in the classroom. Pick, choose, use it all or none – but be sure to enjoy your "year" in Mexico.

¡Buena Suerte!

Sus Amigas (Your friends)

Table of Contents

Incorporating Spanish in Your Classroom

Habían tres ratones y un gato. Un ratón corrío y el gato estaba dando caza al ratón. El ratón dijo' – ¡Eek! ¡Eek! – y el gato le comío.

El según ratón corrío y el gato le estaba dando caza cuando el ratón dijo, – ¡Eek! ¡Eek! – y el gato le comío.

El tercer ratón, que era muy inteligente, corrío y el gato le estaba dando caza cuando el ratón dijo, – ¡Woof! ¡Woof! – y el gato se fué.

El Moral: Es importante ser bilingüe.

Once upon a time, there were three mice and a cat. One mouse ran and the cat was hunting him. The mouse said, "Eek! Eek!" and the cat ate him.

The second mouse ran and the cat was hunting him when the mouse said, "Eek! Eek!" and the cat ate him.

The third mouse, who was very intelligent, ran and the cat was hunting him when the mouse said, "Woof! Woof!" and the cat ran away.

The Moral: It is important to be bilingual.

Author Unknown

Incorporating Spanish in Your Classroom Contents

Map of Mexico

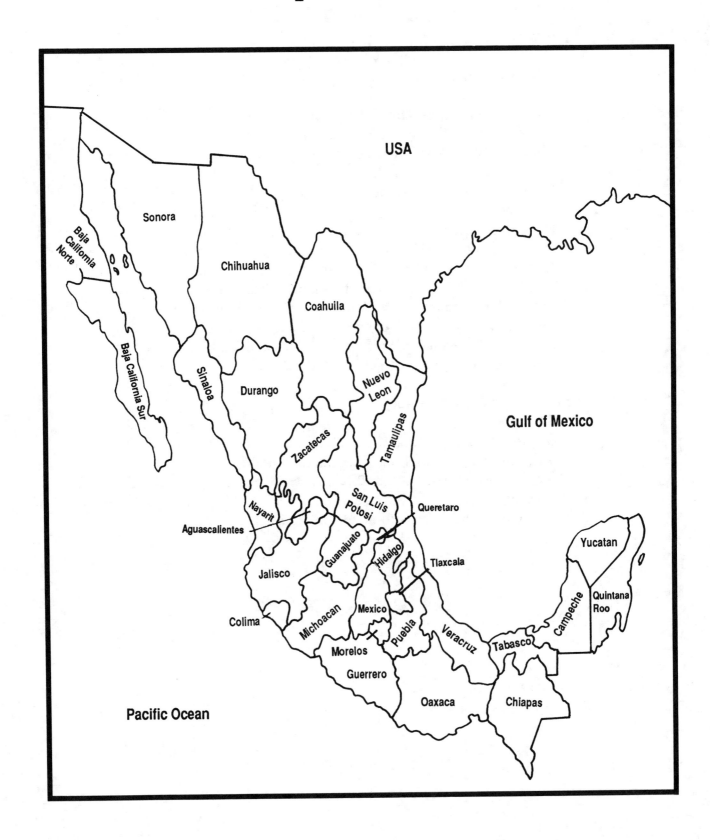

USA

Sonora

Baja California Norte

Chihuahua

Coahuila

Baja California Sur

Sinaloa

Durango

Nuevo Leon

Tamaulipas

Gulf of Mexico

Zacatecas

San Luis Potosi

Queretaro

Nayarit

Aguascalientes

Guanajuato

Hidalgo

Tlaxcala

Yucatan

Jalisco

Mexico

Quintana Roo

Colima

Michoacan

Puebla

Veracruz

Campeche

Morelos

Tabasco

Guerrero

Pacific Ocean

Oaxaca

Chiapas

The Alphabet in Spanish

The alphabet in Spanish has more letters than in English. The English alphabet has 26 and the Spanish alphabet has 30. In learning the correct pronunciation of each letter, you will find that you can read anything in Spanish for the language is very phonetic and follows very definite rules. This, however, does not mean that you will understand what you read but you can sound like a native speaker.

Letters	Sounds of Letters	English Sound	Spanish Word
a	ah	cot	a
b	b	bat	be
c	k or s	cat, city	ce (say)
ch	ch	chin	che
d	d	dog	de
e	eh	pet	e
f	f, ph	foot	efe
g	g, h	go,	ge
h	silent	silent	hache
i	ee	feet	i
j	breathy h	hot	jota
k	k	cake	ka
l	l	lemon	ele
ll	y	yellow	elle
m	m	mind	eme
n	n	no	ene
ñ	n	onion	eñe
o	o	coat	o
p	p	pot	pe
q	ku	cool	cu
r	r	robe	ere
rr	trilled r	not in English	erre
s	s	so	ese
t	t	toe	te
u	oo	cool	u
v	v	vie	ve
w	w	we	doble ve
x	ks	exit	equis
y	y	yellow	i griega
z	s	suit	zeta

The "t" and "d" are pronounced with the tongue slightly between the teeth and not behind the teeth.

Useful Information for the Classroom

The Pledge of Allegiance/El Juramento a la Bandera

Prometo la fidelidad a la bandera
de los Estados Unidos de América,
Y la República que representa,
Una nación, bajo Dios, indivisible,
con libertad y justicia para todos.

Months of the Year/Meses del año
(Note – in Spanish, the months are not capitalized.)

January/enero	July/julio
February/febrero	August/agosto
March/marzo	September/septiembre
April/abril	October/octubre
May/mayo	November/noviembre
June/junio	December/diciembre

Seasons/Estaciones

Summer/verano	Winter/invierno
Spring/primavera	Autumn/otõno

Days of the Week/Días de la semana
(Note – in Spanish the days are not capitalized.)

Sunday/el domingo	Thursday/el jueves
Monday/el lunes	Friday/el viernes
Tuesday/el martes	Saturday/el sábado
Wednesday/el miércoles	

Phrases
¿Cuál es la fecha? (What is the date?)
¿Cuántos días hay en una semana? (How many days in a week?)
¿Qué día es hoy? (What day is it?)
¿En qué estación estamos? (What season is it?)
¡Dígame (díganme-plural) los días de la semana! (Tell me the days of the week!)

Numbers/Números

0	cero	11	once	21	veintiuno
1	uno	12	doce	22	ventidós
2	dos	13	trece	23	ventitrés
3	tres	14	catorce	24	venticuatro
4	cuatro	15	quince	25	veinticinco
5	cinco	16	dieciséis	26	ventiséis
6	seis	17	diecisiete	27	ventisiete
7	siete	18	dieciocho	28	ventiocho
8	ocho	19	diecinueve	29	veintinueve
9	nueve	20	veinte	30	treinta
10	diez				

(Note: The numbers 16 on can also be written as diez y seis, veinte y uno etc.)

Números

Dos y dos son cua-tro   cua-tro y dos son   seis
Seis y dos son o - cho,   y o-cho deis - i -   seis

Child's Song/Canción infantíl

Dos y dos son cuatro, cuatro y dos son seis,
Seis y dos son ocho, y ocho dieciseis.

Two and two are four and two are six,
Six and two are eight, and eight (equals) sixteen.

Family Members/Miembros de la Familia

Mother/Mamá

Father/Papá

Parents/Padres

Uncle/Tío

Aunt/Tía

Cousin/Primo (boy)

       Prima (girl)

Son/Hijo

Daughter/Hija

Children/Hijos (yours)

Woman/Mujer

Man/Hombre

Baby/Bebé

Family/Familia

I/Yo

Family Tree

Grandmother/Abuela

Grandfather/Abuelo

Grandparents/Abuelos

Brother/Hermano

Sister/Hermana

Brother and Sister/Hermanos

Nephew/Sobrino

Niece/Sobrina

Nephew and Niece/Sobrinos

Boy/Muchacho, Niño

Girl/Muchacha, Niña

Youth/Adolescente, joven

Old Woman/Vieja

Old Man/Viejo

Old People/Viejos

El árbol de la familia

Family Tree/El árbol de la familia

Nombre _____

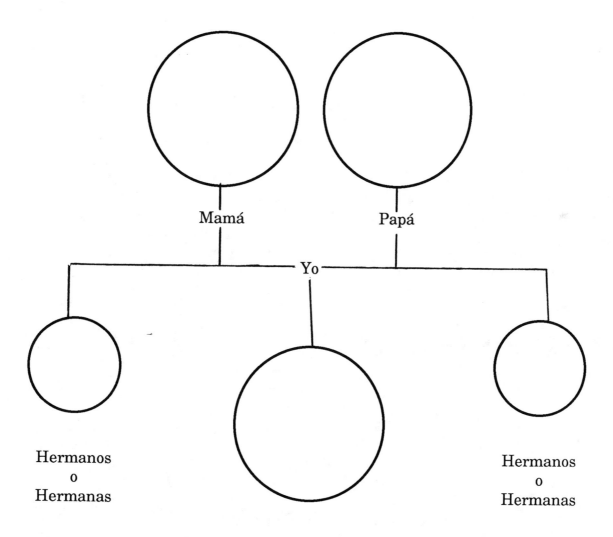

Family Tree/El árbol de la familia

Nombre _____

| abuelo | abuela | abuelo | abuela |

| tíos tias | papá | mamá | tíos tías |

hermanos
o
hermanas   yo   hermanos
o
hermanas

Otros miembros de la familia:
Bisabuelo/bisabuela (great grandfather/mother)
primo/prima (nephew/niece)
padrastro/madrastra (step-father/mother)
hermanastro/hermanastra (step-brother/sister)
hijastro/hijastra (step-son/step-daughter)

El Cuerpo/The Body

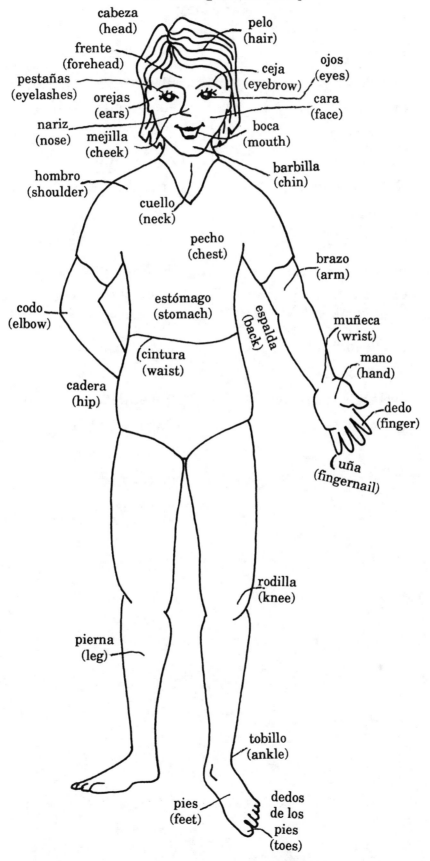

cabeza (head)

pelo (hair)

frente (forehead)

ceja (eyebrow)

ojos (eyes)

pestañas (eyelashes)

orejas (ears)

cara (face)

nariz (nose)

mejilla (cheek)

boca (mouth)

barbilla (chin)

hombro (shoulder)

cuello (neck)

pecho (chest)

brazo (arm)

codo (elbow)

estómago (stomach)

espalda (back)

muñeca (wrist)

cintura (waist)

mano (hand)

cadera (hip)

dedo (finger)

uña (fingernail)

rodilla (knee)

pierna (leg)

tobillo (ankle)

pies (feet)

dedos de los pies (toes)

The Body/El Cuerpo
Vocabulary

HEAD/cabeza

hair/pelo

eye lid/párpado

eyes/ojos

nose/nariz

cheek/mejilla

lip/labio

chin/barbilla

face/cara

ears/orejas

eyebrow/ceja

forehead/frente

mouth/boca

eyelashes/pestañas

BODY/cuerpo

neck/cuello

shoulder/hombro

elbow/codo

hip/cadera

knee/rodilla

leg/pierna

toes/dedos de los pies

back/espalda

stomach/estómago

arm/brazo

waist/cintura

wrist/muñeca

finger/dedo

fingernail/uña

thumb/pulgar

ankle/tobillo

feet/pies

Calendar/Weather Phrases

There are any number of ways that you can incorporate Spanish into your classroom. The easiest way is through the calendar because it is a rote activity and one that is done daily. Some terminology or questions that you might use are as follows:

¡Buenos días! Good morning

¡Buenas tardes! Good afternoon (or evening until the sun goes down)

¡Buenas noches! Good night!

¿Cómo estás? How are you? (addressing one child)

¿Cómo están? How are you all? (addressing more than one)

¡Estoy bien! I am fine.

¡Estoy enfermo! (a) (I am sick) the "o" ending is for a boy and the "a" ending is for
      a girl.

¡Estoy mejor! I am better.

¿Cómo te sientes? How do you feel? (to one child)

¿Cómo se sienten? How do you all feel?

¿Cuál es la fecha? What is the date?

¿Qué día es hoy? What day is it today?

¿Qué día era ayer? What day was it yesterday?

¿Qué tiempo hace hoy? What is the weather like today?

¿Qué día será mañana? What day will it be tomorrow?

¡Hace frío! It is cold!

¡Hace calor! It is hot!

!Hace viento! It is windy!

¡Hay neblina! It is foggy!

¡Está lloviendo! It is raining!

¡Está nevando! It is snowing!

Spanish Vocabulary Games

Step Booklet

Use a regular 8 1/2 x 11 sheet of paper. Cut the paper into three equal columns 2 3/4 x 11 inches. Cut enough columns so that each child receives five (5) sheets. Lay the five sheets on top of each other so that at least one (1) inch is showing of each piece (see diagram). Fold the columns and staple them for a vocabulary book. Write the vocabulary on the chalkboard; for example: un zapato, dos camisas (clothes, etc.)

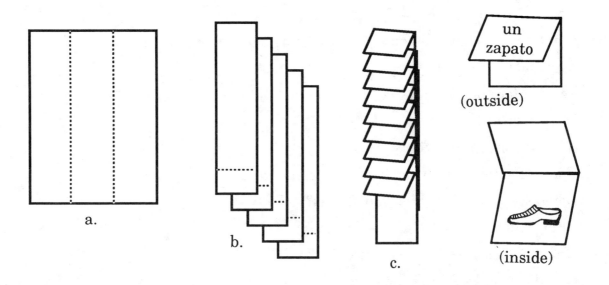

a.

b.

c.

un zapato

(outside)

(inside)

Dot to Dot

Any dot to dot picture can be changed to Spanish by writing the Spanish numbers instead of the English numbers.

uno = 1, dos = 2, tres = 3, cuatro = 4, cinco = 5, seis = 6, siete = 7, ocho = 8, nueve = 9, diez = 10, etc.

Mexican Bingo

It is possible to use regular bingo cards and convert them to Mexican Bingo. Write the words of the vocabulary that you want the children to use on the squares – one word per square. Be sure to write the word on several cards but in different spaces on each card. Also, write the word on a slip of paper that can be drawn to read during the game. Be sure to use beans for your markers!

cero	cinco	dos
ocho	tres	seis
cuatro	siete	uno

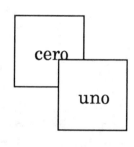

Mexican Memory

Make two sets of cards with vocabulary words on them. Shuffle the cards and put them face down in front of you (as the player). The player may turn over two cards. If the cards match, the player takes the cards and he/she may have another turn. If the two cards do not match, then the two cards are placed face down again in the same places they were taken. The player with the most "pairs" wins.

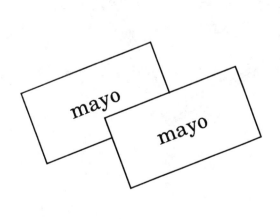

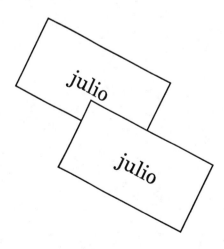

Dictionary
Each child can compile his/her own Spanish dictionary and add new words as they go along.

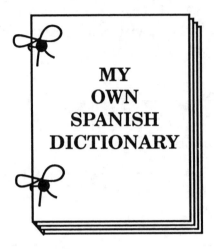

Libro de comida (ropa, nombres etc.)
Individual books can be made. The children find the pictures in magazines and label them with the correct word in Spanish. Catalogues would be particularly helpful with ropa (clothing), muebles (furniture), comida (food), etc. This is also a good exercise for categories.

agosto

AUGUST

THE AZTECS

agosto (August) Contents

August English/Spanish Vocabulary

Aztec	azteca
black	negro (a)
blue	azul
calendar	calendario
circle	círculo
colors	colores
corn	maíz
diamond	diamante
eighth	octavo (a)
fifth	quinto (a)
first	primero (a)
fourth	cuarto (a)
God	Dios
green	verde
Mayans	los Mayo
ninth	noveno (a)
orange	anaranjado (a)
purple	morado (a)
pyramid	pirámide
rectangle	rectángulo
red	rojo (a)
second	segundo (a)
seventh	séptimo (a)
sixth	sexto (a)
square	cuadrado
sun	sol
tenth	décimo (a)
third	tercero (a)
Toltecs	Toltecas
triangle	triángulo
white	blanco (a)
yellow	amarillo (a)

Legend of Quetzalcoatl – The Five Suns

At the beginning of time, the universe was empty and it was without wind and rain, light or life. There was no sun or moon.

There were, however, four sons of the Gods named Red Tzcatlipoca because he was red, the totally black son, Tezcatlipoca, the white son, Quetzalcoatl, and the Blue God, Omitcutli who was born without flesh as a skeleton.

The four sons divided the universe four ways with the Red god ruling the east, north was ruled by the Black god, the Blue god ruled the south and Quetzalcoatl, the white God, ruled the west.

The Red god, being the oldest, appointed the White god and the Blue god to put order into the universe. This made Tezcatlipoca, the Black god, very angry and he swore he would get revenge. He disguised himself as a tiger whose spotted skin resembled the sky and all the stars. Hundreds of years later when man looked up in the sky, they would point to him and call him Ursa Major, the Big Bear except for the Mexicans who knew he was really a tiger. The battle between the Black god and the White god had begun.

Quetzalcoatl made his first creation and put a light up in the sky and created the moon but it was dim so Tezatlipoca rolled himself into a ball and hurled himself into the sky to make the sun. The other gods created the gods of water and they put a huge alligator in the waters. This was the period of the first sun.

Quetzalcoatl struck his brother down from the sky with his staff into the water. The gods had created a race of giants that did nothing but roam the earth and Tezatlipoca disguised himself as a tiger again and devoured all the giants in the darkness.

Quetzalcoatl, the god of the wind, became the second sun but his brother, Tezatlipoca, reached up a claw and pulled Quetzalcoatl from the sky. His fall caused a great hurricane and destroyed all men except a few who became monkeys.

The other brothers became angry with the fighting between the Black and White gods and appointed their own sun who was Tlaloc, the god of rain and heavenly fire. Quetzalcoatl was furious that a minor god was chosen to be the sun so he sent fire onto the earth of such magnitude that those who did not perish were transformed into birds to escape. This was the end of the third sun.

Quetzalcoatl then appointed Chalchihiutlicue to be the fourth sun. This ended with a flood that was sent by Tezcatlipoca. The survivors became fish.

When the waters covered the earth, Quetzalcoatl and Tezatlipoca met. There was no sun and it was dark. The other gods met with them at Teotihuacán to see how they could find the light. Two gods offered to sacrifice themselves – one was rich and one was poor.

A big brazier was heaped with flaming coals and the rich god was to jump into the fire first but every time he got near the rim, he stopped. The poor god closed his eyes and jumped into the fire which hurled him into the sky and he became the sun. The rich god, ashamed, jumped into the fire and was slowly consumed and became the moon. The other gods became angry and threw a rabbit at the moon and that is why the Mexicans see a rabbit on the moon and not the man in the moon as others know it. The rest sacrificed themselves and became stars.

Quetzalcoatl's next mission was to create man. He descended into the lower regions to the gods of death and obtained the bones of men and women who had already died. He broke them into pieces. At the "place of birth," he ground the pieces into ashes and mixed it with the blood of other gods and molded the human as we know them today.

Quetzalcoatl knew now that his people must be fed and a red ant told him about a rare treasure under a hill. Quetzalcoatl followed the red ant and discovered a kernel of corn. He learned also from the ant, all the skills of building, how to organize and develop a civilization, how to make pyramids and create beautiful works of art. Quetzalcoatl passed all these skills on to the humans.

So, in gratitude, the Toltecs and the Aztecs named the White god, Quetzalcoatl – the serpent with beautiful plumes from the quetzal bird. The Mayans called him Kulcan which also means serpent and bird.

However, while Quetzalcoatl taught the people the good things in life, the evil gods taught the people the opposite. For example, the God of Night required they sacrifice humans for if they didn't offer the blood and hearts of the humans to the sun, the light and the warmth of the sun would vanish forever. Quetzalcoatl left the earth in his human form off the east coast of Mexico in the year 1000 according to the legend but he promised he would return to impart more wisdom and knowledge to his people.

NOTE: This is but one version of this legend. There are others that vary.

Early History

Some early dates:

20,000 B.C.	First people in Mexico
7500 B.C.	People were hunters and lived off plants and small animals.
7000 B.C.	People in Puebla area became farmers raising corn, avocados, beans, pepper, squash and tomatoes. They also ate wild turkeys and dogs.
2000 B.C.	Large villages appeared around Lake Texcoco in the south-central valley.
1200 B.C. – 100 B.C.	Olmec Indians flourished on the southern coast. They developed a counting system and calendar.
A.D. 250 - 900	The Classic Period. The pyramids were built and dedicated to the sun and the moon at Teotihuacán. Maya Indians were in the Yucatán Peninsula. Zapotec Indians appeared in Oaxaca.

(The classroom may wish to make a timeline using the above information.)

The Toltecs

The Toltec Indians flourished during the 900's. Their capitol was at Tula, north of the present day Mexico City. The Toltec's invaded the Yucatán peninsula and rebuilt Chichén-Itzá, a Mayan religious community. The main influence of the Toltecs was in the usage of the stone pillars to support the roofs, human sacrifice and the White god, Quetzalcoatl. The Chichimec tribes destroyed the Toltecs and Tula around 1200 B.C.

History of the Aztecs

In the 13th century, the Aztec, or Mexica, Indians came to the Valley of Mexico from their original home on a northern lake island called Aztlán. Although they were a primitive nomadic people, they conquered the other nations of the Valley of Mexico and absorbed many of the existing customs into their own religion, rituals and mythology. The Aztec empire spread throughout the Pacific and Gulf coasts, and from the Isthmus of Tehuantepec north to the Pánuco River.

These black-haired, black-eyed people with coppery brown skins, settled in the valley and made Tenochtitlán their capital. Tenochtitlán was in the center of Lake Texcoco and was an island. Quetzalcoatl had told the people to look for an island where there was an eagle sitting on top of a cactus with a serpent in his mouth. When the Aztecs saw this wondrous sight at Tenochtitlán, they knew the gods had sent it to them. This site is now know as Mexico City and this happening is observed on the national flag of Mexico. Tenochtitlán had a population of about 100,000 when the Spaniards arrived in 1519.

The city had palaces and parks, a water system, fountains and many winding canals. The men hunted or fished, worked the silver and gold, served in the army or tilled the soil.

Cotton was also cultivated. They used a kind of century plant called maguey which was grown for its fiber, which was woven into clothing and made into sandals. Its juice was made into a drink. Their chief crop was corn (maiz), but they also had beans, squashes, tomatoes, sweet potatoes, chili peppers and many fruits.

They also planted orchards of cocoa for making chocolate. They also used the beans for money.

The Aztecs were fierce warriors who believed it was their duty to sacrifice the men they captured in battle to their gods. The people they conquered hated the Aztecs because of the sacrifice of the thousands of prisoners that occurred.

These early Mexicans, or Aztecs, worshipped the sun and the moon and many other gods. Since they were an agricultural nation, they worshipped the gods that would directly favor a good crop such as rain, fertility, a bountiful crop etc.

One of their most important gods was Quetzelcoatl which meant "bird serpent" or "feathered snake." The Aztecs believed that Quetzelcoatl would some day come back to earth as a fair-skinned white man with long hair and a flowing beard.

When the Aztecs believed that their gods were angry with them, they made human sacrifices to gain back their favor. They also prayed to all the other gods as they went about their daily lives. They prayed to the gods of the seeds that they would multiply and grow. They prayed to the gods of the soil that they would accept the seeds. The god of rain was prayed to, to bring water to nourish the crops and so forth.

Little boys of six or eight years were sent off to a boarding school and seldom saw their parents. Girls learned to spin and weave, to cook, to serve meals and to write and tell stories. The girls also went to a girl's school that was not as strict as the boys.

The Aztec mothers spun cloth and wove it, dyed cloth, made clothes of feathers or rabbit skins and cooked the food. The same corn pancakes – tortillas – were served just the way they are made today.

Moctezuma was the ruler of the Aztec nation and he lived in a very beautiful palace. He wore beautiful cloaks of fine cloth which were trimmed with precious jewels. He also wore robes of beautiful feathers or furs from the rabbit or jaguar. The soles of his sandals were made of gold. When he left the palace, he was always carried on a jeweled litter for his feet were never to touch the bare ground.

Even though Columbus never saw the natives in Mexico, he gave them a name that has been used ever since because when Columbus landed in San Salvador, Cuba and Haiti, he thought he had reached India and so he called the people he found there, Indios (Indians).

Hernán Cortés

The Spaniards began to occupy the West Indies during the 1490's which eventually led to the discovery of Mexico in 1517. The governor of Cuba, Diego Velázquez, sent ships with Francisco Fernández de Córdoba to explore the west and to look for treasure. Córdoba found the Yucatán Peninsula and brought back stories of large cities and many treasures.

Reports also filtered back to the Aztec chief, at that time, Moctezuma II, in Tenochtitlán. The stories told of white, bearded men with strange animals (horses) with loud weapons that killed. Surely these men were gods.

A third expedition of about 550 Spaniards sailed from Cuba under Hernando Cortés or Hernán Cortés.

Hernán Cortés, a man of limited military experience, landed at Veracruz on the coast of Mexico on Good Friday, 1519. Imagine the surprise when he was met by ambassadors of Montezuma (Moctezuma) II laden with lavish gifts of gold, silver, turquoise, rich textiles, colorful plumes or feathers and furs. It is no wonder that Hernán Cortés wanted to go to Tenochtitlán to meet this chief in person. It was a journey that would take him more than 83 days to travel the more than 400 miles. He and his men would have to travel from 0 (zero) elevation to more than 12,000 feet across three series of mountains.

Hernán Cortés was about 34 years old when he began this extraordinary journey. He was willing to take great risks but he also proved himself an exceptional diplomat for he was able to win over many members of other tribes that hated the Aztecs for their sacrificial practices. Cortés was a very religious man and was disgusted with the sacrifices and the religious practices of the natives. Yet, he could be very ruthless himself; for example, in the city of Cholula, he killed 3,000 warriors.

Cortés' orders had been to "explore" and not to take any unnecessary risks. He had no authority to travel into the Valley of Mexico to meet the Aztecs. Cortés squelched the opposition among his own men by hanging two of his men, flogging others and destroying his entire fleet.

Cortés left 150 men at Villa Rica and took most of his soldiers, the sailors from the wrecked ships, a few Indian servants from Cuba and led by 400 Totonac warriors and bearers from Mexico, he began his journey to meet Moctezuma II.

A remarkable event permitted the Spaniards to communicate with the Indians. On the Yucatán Peninsula, Cortés took some slaves, one of which was a beautiful young woman whose native language was Náhuatl, the Aztec language. Her Indian name was Malinalli but the Spaniards baptized her Marina. Cortés spoke Spanish to Aquilar, who spoke maya to Doña Marina who spoke Nahuatl to the Aztecs. Doña Marina was so effective and worked so well with Cortés, that the two of them were associated together by the Indians. She became known as Malintzin which became Malinche to the Mexicans. She is said to have born Cortés a son.

Cortés' journey is recorded by Bernal Díaz del Castillo. Mexico emphasizes its Indian heritage and, therefore, there are few if any official memorials to Cortés.

Cortés and his men were involved with heavy battles with the Tlaxcalan warriors but with neither side a victor, they agreed on an alliance and eventually it was this tribe that would help Cortés conquer the Aztecs.

It was at Cholula, the sacred city of Quetzelcoatl that Cortés met with the Aztecs in battle. Doña Marina, who had become an advisor to Cortés, warned him of a large force of Aztecs camped nearby. At dawn, the Spaniards could see the warriors entering the plazas and at a signal, Cortés wrote, "we fell upon the Indians in such fashion that within two hours more than three thousand of them lay dead." This is why in Mexico today that Doña Marina is know as La Malinche, the traitor.

After this battle, Cortés received no more interference from the natives on his way to Tenochtitlán and Moctezuma II. "And this was our venturesome and daring entry into the great city of Tenochtitlán Mexico, the eighth day of November, the year of our Savior Jesus Christ one thousand, five hundred and nineteen." It was the beginning of the end for the Aztecs.

Soon after Cortés entered the city, he imprisoned Moctezuma. Six months later he left to confront a Spanish army at Cempoala, sent by the angry government of Cuba. Cortés defeated this army and pressed them into service. When he returned to Tenochtitlán, he found the natives in revolt and they stoned and killed their leader, Moctezuma. The Spaniards recaptured the city of Tenochtitlán on August 13, 1521 and began the building of New Spain there on the ruins of the pyramids, palaces and buildings of the Aztecs. The present day Zocolo (the center of present day Mexico City) is built over the ruins of Moctezuma's palace.

The Aztec Cosmos

Illustration from, The Axtec Cosmos, Teoilhuicatlapaluaztli-Ollin Tonalmachiotl The Great and Venerable Mechanism of the Universe. Illustrated with Glyphs from Pre-Columbian Codices and Reliefs. Traced and Collected by Tomas J. Filsinger. Published by Celestial Arts, Berkeley, California. Copyright ©1984. Reprinted with permission.

The Aztec Calendar

In the 13th century, the Aztec, or Mexica, Indians came to the Valley of Mexico from their original home called Atzlán. Their gods had told them to look for an island in a lake with an eagle on a cactus with a serpent in his mouth. They found just this spot at Tenochtitlán in Lake Texcoco as the gods had foretold.

Their civilization flourished until it was conquered by a Spanish explorer named Hernán Cortés. The buildings were destroyed and the present day Mexico City has been built on their ruins.

On December 17, 1790, workers were excavating near the center of Mexico City, when a huge twenty-six ton face was found buried face down. A face that, at one time, had been at the corner of the ceremonial center of the Aztec's capital, Tenochtitlán. It can now be seen in the National Museum of Anthropology and History in Chapultepec Park in Mexico City.

Many of the Indians were converted to Catholicism; however, the old customs and beliefs were hard to erase. Perhaps that is why the archbishop pushed the people to bury this tremendous sculpture.

Since this stone was discovered, it has been the most studied and written about example of Mesoamerican art.

It is more commonly known as the Aztec Calendar or the Sun Stone.

The Aztecs believed that the end of the world would come at the end of a 52-year cycle. According to the legend, four suns have been destroyed by different catastrophes. The center of the stone is the fifth sun, Tonatiuh, the present era.

The Aztecs did not have an alphabet as we know it. Rather, they used letters or sign to stand for the sounds of language. These signs are called hieroglyphs or glyphs to represent an idea. It is much easier to understand the glyphs for concretes objects but it is much harder to understand abstract ideas and concepts.

INNERMOST CIRCLE

In the center of the stone is Tonatiuh with the mask of fire. He is the King of the Planets. He was shown with blond hair for his golden aspect and wrinkle to show his advanced years. The sign "ome acatl" on his forehead refers to the beginning of the year count or "Xiuhmolpilli" that is, the first day of the 52-year cycle after the night when the fire is rekindled. The tongue out, in the form of an obsidian knife, shows his need for human blood and hearts. The beads were thought to be a symbol of the sacred cycle.

SECOND CIRCLE: OLLIN MOVEMENT

The four cardinal points are represented in this circle. The warrior's head-dress indicates the NORTH. The dagger "tecpatl" symbolizes EAST. The house of the god of rain and celestial fire "Tlalocan" is WEST and SOUTH is represented by the monkey.

Other glyphs:

4 Jaguar: "Ocelotonatiuh" During that era, giants lived that had been created by the gods but were devoured by the jaguars.

4 Wind: "Ehecatl" The crocodile head. During this period, the human race was destroyed by high winds and hurricanes and men were converted into monkeys.

4 Rain: The head of rain and celestial fire. Everything was destroyed by lava and fire and men turned into birds to escape the catastrophe.

4 Water: "Chalchiuhtlicue" the water goddess, wife of Tlaloc. The torrential rains came and man turned into fish to keep from drowning.

The rounded part on both sides contain the hand of the god armed with eagle claws crushing the human hearts and signifying the need for sacrifices so that the sun might continue its course.

THIRD CIRCLE: THE TWENTY DAYS

There are twenty boxes with the day signs which are read beginning with the upper left box. The twenty days were counted by fives with each fifth day being a market day or "tianquiztli." Since the five "nemontemi" were useless, it meant that there were 72 market days in the year, days of fiesta or rest, and 288 working days. The ritual calendar consisted of 260 days, divided into twenty periods of 13 days each and the combination of two calendars resulted in the 52 year cycle.

DAYS

First Day:	"Cipactli" (Crocodile)
Second Day:	"Ehecatl" (Wind)
Third Day:	"Calli" (House)
Fourth Day:	"Cuetzpallin" (Lizard)"
Fifth Day:	"Coatl" (Serpent)
Sixth Day:	"Miquiztli" (Death)
Seventh Day:	"Mazatl" (Deer)
Eighth Day:	"Tochtli" (Rabbit)
Ninth Day:	"Atl" (Water)
Tenth Day:	"Itzcuintli" (Dog)
Eleventh Day:	"Ozomtli" (Monkey)
Twelfth Day:	"Malinalli" (Plant, grass)
Thirteenth Day:	"Acatl" (Reed)
Fourteenth Day:	"Ocelotl" (Jaguar)
Fifteenth Day:	"Cuauhtli" (Eagle)
Sixteenth Day:	"Cozacuauhtli" (Vulture)
Seventeenth Day:	"Ollin" (Movement)
Eighteenth Day:	"Tecpatl" (Flint or obsidian)
Nineteenth Day:	"Quiahuitl" (Rain)
Twentieth Day:	"Xochitl" (Flower)

The arrowheads pointing in all directions represent the sun's rays scattering throughout the universe.

The tiny oval shapes ending in a point are the drops of blood offered to the sun god.

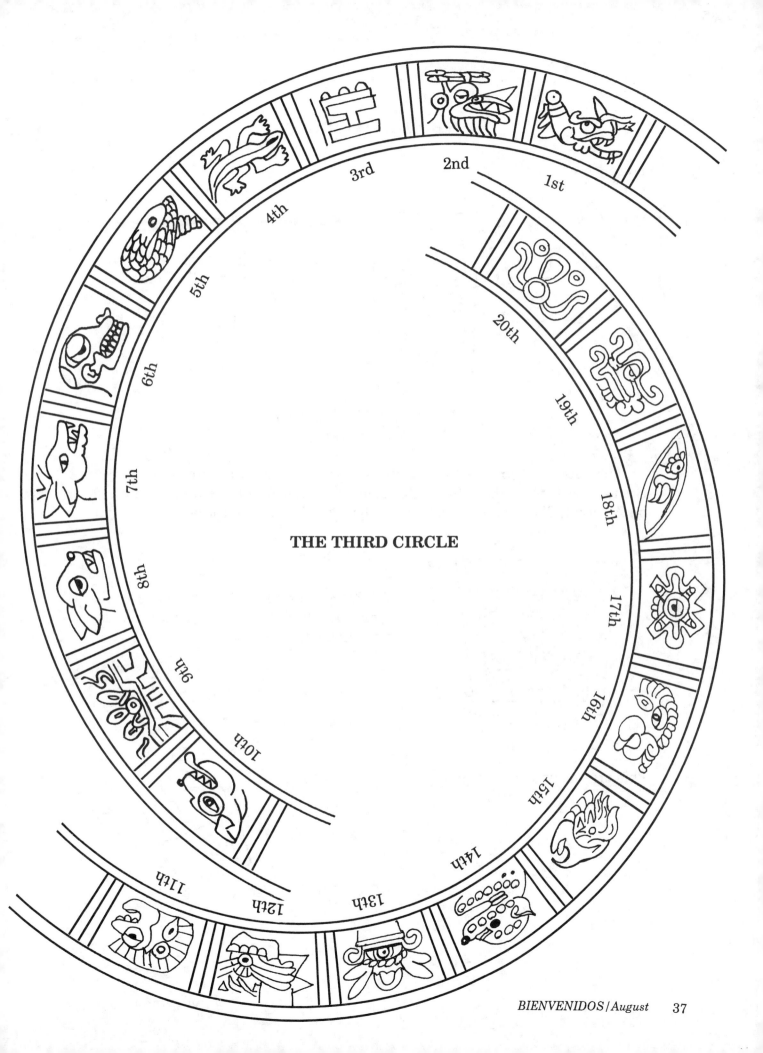

THE THIRD CIRCLE

1st
2nd
3rd
4th
5th
6th
7th
8th
9th
10th
11th
12th
13th
14th
15th
16th
17th
18th
19th
20th

THE THIRD CIRCLE

a. five-in-five days
b. adornment of the sun
c. sun-rays
d. drops of human blood

THE OUTERMOST CIRCLE
(Xiuhcoatis)

The outermost circle is the two bodies of fire serpents who surround the Sun Stone or Aztec Calendar. They are Quetzelcoatl, shown as Tonatiuh, the sun god, on the right. The other is Tezctlipoca, shown as Xiuhtecutli, the god of the night.

The "glyph" of 13-reed corresponds to the year 1479, the date that the Aztec Calendar was finished.

This ornament signifies light, power, and beauty.

The straight bars mean fire and the flames represent the new fire, rekindled every 52 years.

The outside edge of the border shows the milky way with all the circles.

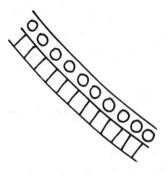

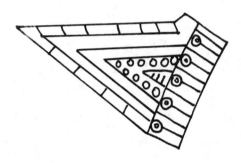

On both sides of the hieroglyph, 13-reed, descend two fire serpents who transport the sun through the universe. They are across from Tonatiuh and Xiuhtecutli.

The two groups of four tied bands of "amatl" (paper made from bark) are the four groups of thirteen years that go together to make 52 years.

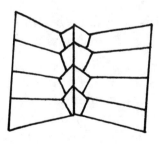

The bodies of the serpents are divided into eleven equal parts which can be seen in the flames.

Aztec Writing

The Aztecs were very organized and not only kept records of their trade but they also kept all the records of the locations and numbers of their population. The scribes were expected to register all births and deaths, list the rulers, festivals and religious rites, the calendar and the laws. All these facts were recorded on a codex, which were strips of paper made from the maguey cactus or deerskin folded like a screen.

The sad part of history is that many of these recordings of history were destroyed by the Spanish after the Conquest.

The Aztecs did not have an alphabet but they did have a system of recording information known as hieroglyphics. This is a system of using "glyphs" or symbols for words.

The Aztecs sold things by the number and not by weight. For example, a "troje" was equal to a bin of 200 tons and "tlacopintli" was equal to a bin that held about 235-140 pounds.

The way they measured was according to the span of a man's hand. Another measure was the length of a man's arm and still another was the height of a man from the ground to as high as the man could reach.

Trade was done by the barter system with the cocoa bean used as currency for smaller items; however, goose quills filled with gold dust or cloth were used as well.

The Aztec calendar was very similar to that of the Mayans. It was based on a number system of one to thirteen and a cycle of 20 name days. It could be divided into four or five equal parts. A list of twenty deities was associated with each cycle of thirteen days called the Lords of the Day and another thirteen deities called the Lords of the Night.

The Aztec solar year was carried over from the Mayans in that it consisted of 365 days divided into eighteen named months, each month being made up of 20 days. The additional five days (nemontemi) didn't belong to a month as they were "unlucky" days. The year was named for the sacred day on which the year began. An example would be, "Fall of the Waters." etc. The calendar decided the festivals which occurred each month. The new year was celebrated by lighting a new fire.

The numbers had a vigesimal system; that is, they counted by twenties. One to 19 were written as dots, 20 was written as a flag, 20 x 20 was written as a feather or fig tree and 20 x 20 x 20 was written as a bag or pouch.

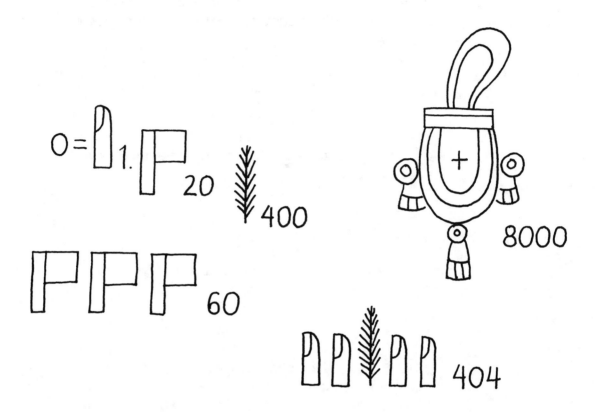

How is Mayan arithmetic alike?

How is Mayan arithmetic different?

Would you like to use Aztec math or Mayan math instead of the numbers we use today? Why or why not?

Suggested Activities

Make an Aztec Calendar
The Three Circles of the Aztec Calendar can be colored, cut-out and pasted together to make their own Sun Stone.

Hieroglyphics
Develop your own set of "hieroglyphics" making a code and use the code to send messages, to give the correct answer for an assignment etc.

Pyramids
Build your own pyramids with different sized boxes and paint them.

Sign Language
Be creative: sign language is another use of symbols in place of words. Are there other people who use symbols for language? (hint: Japanese, Indians etc.)

My Own Personal Hieroglyphic Calendar

You will need three circles:

1. Divide the largest ring into twelve different parts.

2. Using one section for each month, design and draw a symbol for each month in the largest circle. Example: January might be a snowman, February a heart, March a shamrock, April an umbrella, May a flower, June a pair of sunglasses, July a firecracker, August a sun or fall leaf, September a book, October a Jack-O-Lantern, November a turkey and December a Santa Claus.

3. The middle-sized calendar could be divided into seven (7) days. Again, decide on symbols for each day and fill in each division. Each child may have something different due to scouting, lessons, etc.

4. The center could be another symbol for the year. Why is 1990, for example, an important year?

(Use pattern on following page.)

My Own Personal Hieroglyphic Calendar

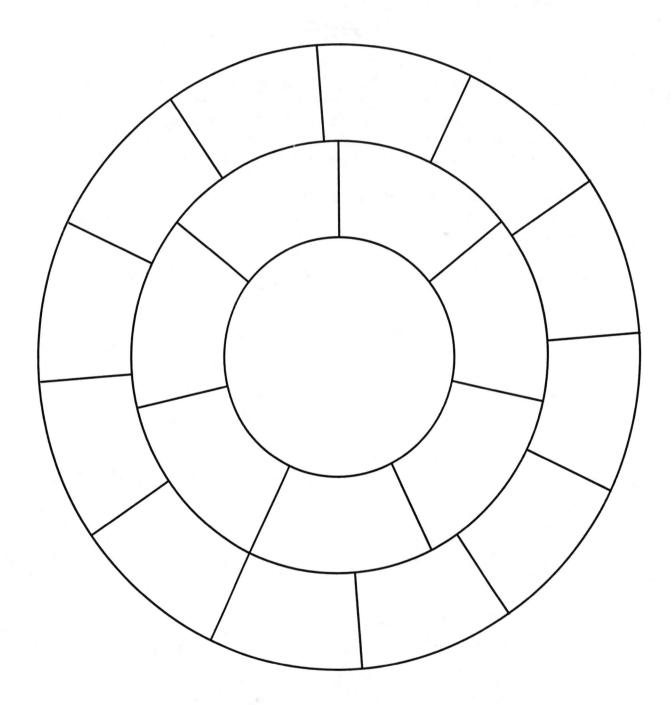

Peep Box

1. Using an old shoe box, cut a hole at one end of the box. Cut a larger hole in the lid of the box. (You have to let some light in so you can see.)

2. Build an Aztec village in the box using construction paper, twigs, tag board, clay etc.

3. Put the cover on top of the box and look through the round hole. A three-dimensional village.

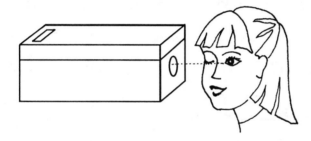

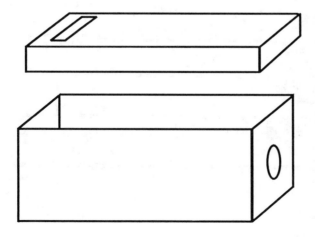

Pyramid Silhouettes

Imagine yourself coming through the jungle and you see the Aztec village with those beautiful pyramids at sunset. The pyramids are black against a magnificent Mexican sunset.

1. Do a water color wash using reds and oranges and let it dry on a large pieces of white construction paper.

2. As an alternative, you might want to finger paint the background.

3. After the paint has dried, glue on pyramids that have been cut out of black construction paper. Add cactus or whatever the imagination will allow.

Silver Necklace

Some of the Aztec designs are still used by many of the artists in Mexico today. Included is a suggestion for a "silver" necklace using the primitive designs of the Aztecs.

1. It is possible here to use some of the designs from the Aztec Calendar. Trace a design on a piece of cardboard and cut it out.

2. Cut the pieces of cord and glue them on the outlines of the design. *Make it simple!*

3. Take a piece of aluminum foil **larger** than the cutout and gently mold it around the cord by pressing down around the cord.

4. After the pattern is secure, tuck the edges of the foil in the back and glue it to the cardboard.

5. Punch a hole at the top and wear your "silver" necklace with pride.

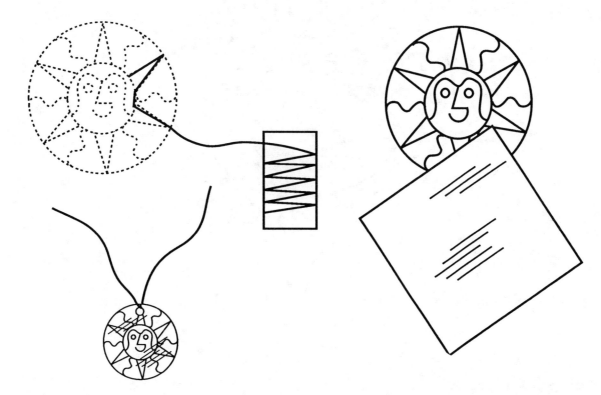

Aztec Mask

1. Use 1/2 of a paper plate cut in half or 3/4ths of a white paper plate (for older children with larger faces).

2. Cut out the holes for eyes and one for the nose. Be sure to measure them on the face before you cut. This is an opportunity for children to work in pairs but caution the children to measure where the eyes and nose are with a pencil.

3. Adorn your masks or paint them as the imagination permits. Use feathers, glitter, fabric, beads etc.

septiembre

SEPTEMBER

NEW SPAIN
INDEPENDENCE

septiembre (September) Contents

September English/Spanish Vocabulary

banner	la bandera
city	la ciudad
country	el país
county	el condado
democracy	la democracía
eagle	el águila
flag	la bandera
flowers	las flores
government	el gobierno
governor	el gobernador
law	la ley
mayor	el alcalde
paper	el papel
party	la fiesta
politician	el político
president	el presidente
serpent	culebra, serpiente
square	plaza (as in a city square)
The state of	el estado de
The United States of America	Los Estados Unidos de América

New Spain History

Colombus' voyage in 1492 marked the beginning of Spain's influence in the New World. Colombus' persistence with the governments of Spain and Portugal in pursuing a new western route to Cipangu, Japan, enabled him to successfully launch a voyage to the wealthy and mysterious land described by Marco Polo. Thirty three days after they set sail to the west, Colombus' band of 90 men and boys reached the island of San Salvador in the Bahamas. This was hardly the destination Colombus expected and, at the time, the voyage was considered a failure, Nevertheless, it signalled the birth of European expansion in the New World.

In 1493 Pope Alexander IV divided the world of discovery between Spain and Portugal at a line 100 leagues west of the Azores and the Cape Verde Islands. All new discoveries to the west of the line belonged to Spain, all those to the east, would belong to Portugal. This declaration fanned the fires of expansion and exploration.

The conquest of the Caribbean was carried out by Spanish conquistadores. These were not professional military men, but lower gentry or *hidalgos*. Many were skilled artisans, carpenters, or shipbuilders. They came looking for gold, personal glory, or with a religious mission. They had no real military training or rank. It was only a matter of time until the conquests of the Caribbean area led to the conquest of Mexico.

Hernández de Córdoba and Diego Velázquez both sailed to Mexico at the beginning of the 16th century and came back with stories of a great civilization. The leadership of the Mexican conquest would fall to Hernán Cortés, who served with Velázquez while he was governor in Cuba. Cortés was born in Extremadura, an area in Spain from which many conquistadores came. He studied law for a short time at the University of Salamanca, but enjoyed adventure and sailed to the New World when he was nineteen. He was an astute trader and built a fortune for himself by the time he was 30.

Cortés sailed for Mexico with 550 men, 11 ships and 16 horses. His fleet landed at Tabasco and immediately defeated the town. Cortés received Doña Marina or Malinche from the Tabascans as part of his tribute. She became his translator and mistress. Cortés sailed to Veracruz, then marched inland with his men to Tenochtitlán. Cortés met little resistance as he traveled. Many Indians believed he was the God Quetzalcoatl returning to them.

The Spaniards were able to move in and conquer the Indians so quickly because they brought with them weapons unknown to the Indian population. They had horses to move their men and supplies. The Indians, who had never seen these magnificent animals, were frightened by their power and speed. They also had firearms, which the Indians believed gave these white men god-like control of thunder and lightening. Probably the most horrible weapon the conquistadores brought with them was disease. By the end of the conquest in 1521, many thousands of Indians had died from smallpox, a disease heretofore unknown in Mexico.

After Cortés' conquest, Spain set about establishing economic and governmental controls over her new land. *The Casa de Contratación*, or House of Trade regulated commerce in the colonies. The cities were the focal points of activity, as they were in Spain. New World cities were set up via the Spanish model, with a central *plaza*, surrounded by important public buildings, the church, and the homes of wealthy residents. Also, like Spain, the major cities were located inland.

The new land was governed by a Viceroy, who was the personal representative of the crown and had all the privileges of a sovereign. The Viceroy was advised by the *audiencia*, whose members had certain executive and legislative powers. The most important organization for local control was the *ayuntamiento*, or town council. The governmental system was supported by the *quinto*, royal fifth of all treasure, paid by those who controlled Indian labor. These controls led to the *mordida*, literally the bite, or bribe as a common practice among public officials.

The *encomienda* system came to be the meeting place between the two cultures. The encomienda was a grant of Indian labor and tribute usually awarded to someone who had given extraordinary governmental or military service to the crown. The *encomendero* also received a small grant of land, *la estancia*. The laws of the encomienda were designed to protect the rights of the Indians but the encomenderos did not always observe those laws, and the priests often acted as intermediaries in these situations. The encomienda system would be replaced with another tenure system of land distribution after Independence in 1821, the *hacienda*.

The encomiendas provided a place for Spaniards and Indians to share lifestyles, art, food, music, and bloodlines. Even though economics and profession played an important part in one's social standing, bloodline nomenclatures were written into the law. There were over 100 different nomenclatures. The more common were: *peninsular*; pure Spaniard born in Spain, *criollo*; pure Spaniard born in the New World, *mestizo*; Indian and Spaniard, *zambo*; Black and Indian, and often all mixed castes were called *castas de mezcla*. The mestizo was subjected to much prejudice during the colonial period.

Professions such as physicians, lawyers, and the clergy, were all deemed to be deserving of respect and were entitled to hold the rank of *hidalgo*.

Vocabulary for New Spain

Cristóbal Colón – Sailed under the flag of Spain to San Salvador in 1492 while searching for a route to the orient.

Cipangu – Marco Polo's Japan.

Inter Caetera – Papal bull by Alexander IV which divided the world, 1493.

San Salvador – Watling's Island, coral reef in the Bahamas where Colombus first landed.

Hernán Cortés – Spanish conquistador, conquered Tenochtitlan in 1521.

Diego Velázquez – Governor of Cuba, friend of Cortés – sent Cortés to Mexico, then revoked his commission.

Tabascanos – Mayan speaking people – fought bravely, horses decided battle.

Náhuatl – native language of the Aztecs.

Virrey – Vicery Assistant King in the New World. Had all the accouterments of a king.

mordida – the payoff, literally, the bite.

audiencia – advisory body to the viceroy.

ayuntamiento – town council.

quinto real – royal fifth, 20 percent of all treasure paid to the crown.

encomienda – a grant of Indians for their labor and tribute to an encomendero.

estancia – a grant of land.

ciudades – cities.

mayordomo – estate manager of the encomienda.

hacienda – system of land ownership and "free market" Indian labor which was born after the demise of the encomienda system.

peninsular (gachupín) – pure blood Spaniard born in Spain.

criollo – a person born of a "pure blood" Spaniard born in the New World.

mestizo – Indian and Spanish blood.

zambo – Black and Indian blood.

Mulatto – a mixture of Spanish and Black.

Don or Doña – titles of rank equivalent to Sir and Lady.

hidalgo – rank of lower gentry similar to squire, literally "hijo de algo" or son of something.

Malinche – became Cortés' mistress and interpreter.

Independence

During the beginning of the 19th century, the idea of independence was discussed among some of the progressive lawyers and priests of the day. In 1808 the Viceroy was removed by a group of peninsulares in a bloodless coup. The areas of Guanajuato and Queretaro were mining regions, and it was here that a more aggressive stance toward independence developed because of the treatment toward the Indians in the mines. There was also a small group of intellectuals who formed the Querétaro Society, and provided leadership for a revolutionary movement.

The priest Miguel Hidalgo y Costilla was rector of the College in Morelia and a member of the Querétaro Society. The priest was involved with teaching the Indians and believed along with the other intellectuals in the society that they had a right to Independence. This group of disenchanted criollos plotted a strike against the peninsular government to take place on October 1, 1810. Their plan was discovered on September 15, and they decided to hastily proceed with their plan. On September 16, 1810 Father Hidalgo rang the bells of the church and challenged his parishioners to regain the rights which had been taken from them by the Spanish 300 years before. So began the patriots fight for liberty with "El Grito de Dolores." On October 19, 1810, Father Hidalgo abolished slavery and the payment of tribute for the Indian.

Mexico's first Declaration of Independence and Constitution was adopted by the Congress of Chipancingo in 1814. Father Morelos, a mestizo priest and intellectual, continued the leadership of the Independence movement after the capture and death of Father Hidalgo. The Constitutional army was no match for the Viceroy's forces however, and Father Morelos was also captured and executed in 1815.

The Independence movement had begun and the complete authority Spain had enjoyed earlier would never be possible again.

Vocabulary for Independence

Father Miguel Hidalgo y Costilla – priest of the Church of Dolores, considered the Father of Mexican Independence. Gave the "Grito de Dolores" on September 16, 1810, which called for Independence and equality.

Querétaro Society – This group of intellectuals plotted revolution. Members included Doña María Josefa Ortiz Domínguez, wife of the Corrigidor; Captain Ignacio Allende of the Viceroy's forces; Juan Aldama, the Paul Revere of Mexico; and Father Hidalgo.

Father José María Morelos y Pavón – A mestizo and student of Hidalgo, he took over the leadership of the revolution after the death of Father Hidalgo.

Congress of Chilpancingo – They wrote the Declaration of Independence for Mexico in 1813 and a Constitution in 1814.

The Eagle

The eagle is a national symbol in Mexico. Color the eagle and serpent, cut them out and cut in the beak to hold the serpent and hang as a mobile. Be sure to color both sides.

Construction Paper Flag of Mexico

The Mexican Flag is comprised of three colors: white for religion, green for independence and red for unity. In the center of the flag is an eagle with a serpent in its mouth. Hundreds of years ago, the Aztecs were led through the legend of their gods, to a land where they would see, sitting on a cactus, an eagle with a serpent in his mouth. They saw this eagle in a land that the Aztec's called Tenochtitlan and they built their capital on that spot. Mexico City is now built on that very spot.

Materials:
White drawing paper – 9" x 12", red construction paper 4" x 9", green construction paper 4" x 9", copy of the eagle, stapler, crayons or markers, glue

1. Glue the green and red construction paper to the white paper. The green on your left and the red to your right.

2. Cut out the eagle and glue or staple it to the center.

Mexican Flag

Make copies of the included flag of Mexico *(found on page 62)* and distribute them to the children. Have them color them and glue the following salute or poem to the back.

Bandera de colores
yo te doy mi corazón
te saludo mi bandera
con respeto y con amor.

Es el saludo de un niño
que siempre ha de ver en tí
algo grande y respetado
bandera de mi país.

Rosaura Zapata

Flag of three colors
I give you my heart
I salute my flag
with respect and love.

It is the salute of a child
that always makes one see in you
something great and respected
Flag of my country.

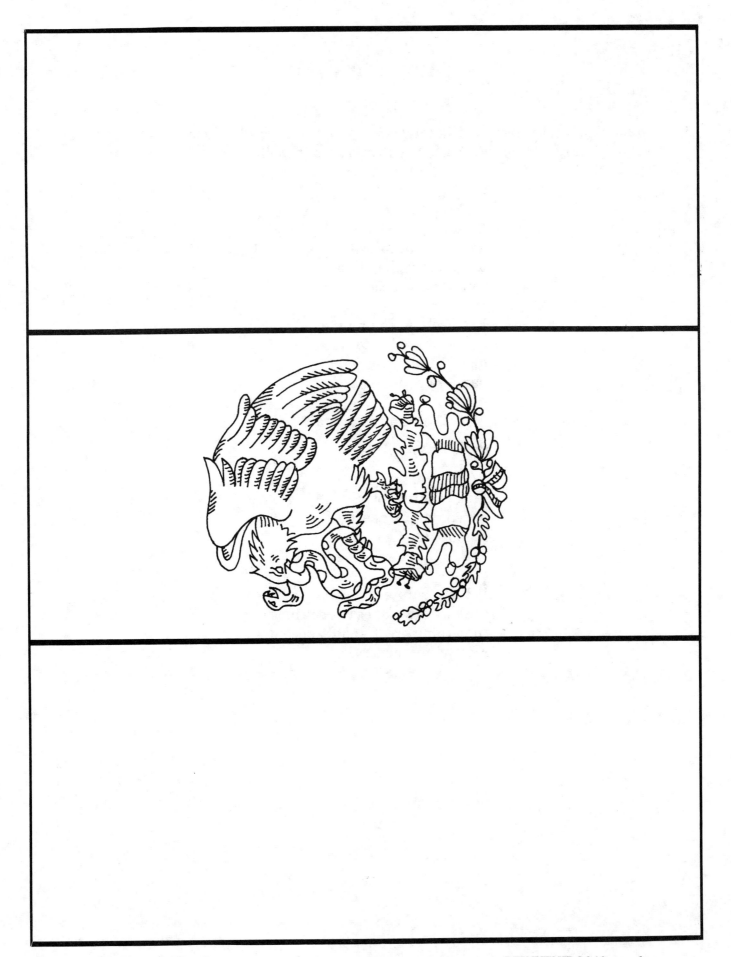

Mexican Poetry

Saludo a La Bandera

Bandera de tres colores
        yo te doy mi corazón
te saludo mi bandera
        con respeto y con amor.

Es el saludo de un niño
        que siempre ha de ver en tí
algo grande y respetado
        bandera de mi país.

        Rosaura Zapata

Salute to the Flag

Flag of three colors
        I give you my heart
I salute you my flag
        With respect and love.

It is the pledge of a child
        That should always be in you
Something great and respected
        Flag of my country.

        Rosaura Zapata

Septiembre

Septiembre, mes de la patria
        con gusto te veo llegar,
ya que todas nuestras glorias
        nos vienes a recordar

Al sonar de los clarines
        y al redoble del tambor,
te saludamos septiembre
        llenos de pátrio amor.

September

September, month of the native land
        I see you come with joy
You come to remind of all the wonderful
        Things we are.

Upon the sound of the trumpets
        And the beat of the drum
We salute you September
        Filled with patriotic love.

Septiembre

Septiembre, el mexicano
        con gusto lo ve llegar
ya que todas sus glorias
        le viene a recordar

        L. Serradel

September

September, the Mexican
        Sees you come with joy
To remind him of
        All the wondrous things he is.

        L. Serradel

Banners

What good is a fiesta without decorations? In Mexico, people decorate with banners. Hang your Mexican flags, colorful pictures and tissue paper flowers but don't forget your banners.

Materials:
You will need packages of brightly colored tissue paper, scissors and string to hang them.

1. Cut the package into thirds.

2. Cut the paper as shown and be sure not to cut all the way through to the other side.

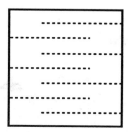

3. Open the paper and carefully hang them to complete your celebration.

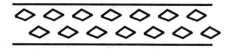

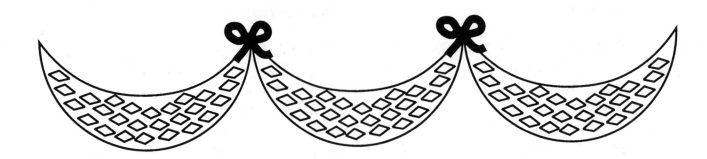

Serpent

Materials:
Construction paper, scissors and crayons and scissors

1. Use a light colored piece of construction paper.

2. Draw a snake that winds its way across the paper.

3. Color the snake or make designs all along his body.

4. Cut out the snake and mount it on the other paper or color both sides and hang it as a mobile.

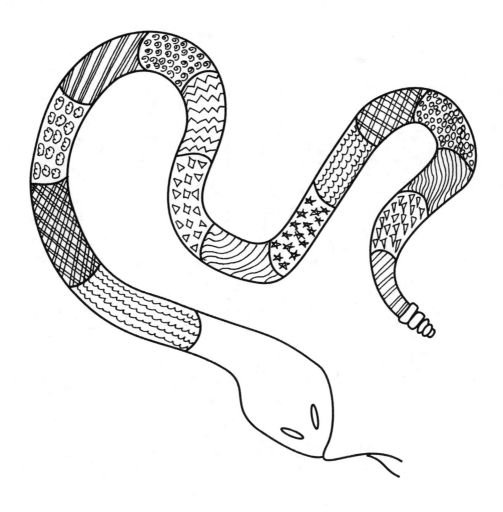

Traditional Dress-Up

1. Complete the figure as a:

    a. Peninsular or criollo

    b. Mestizo

    c. Mulato

    d. Indian

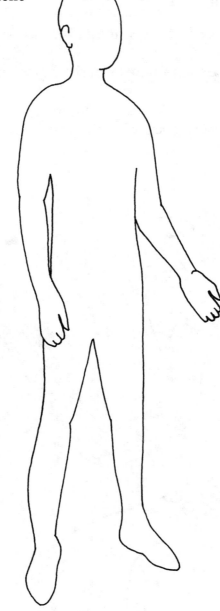

Divide the class into groups to discuss and complete the figure.

What is in his/her hand? Draw it.

Create a Plaza

Materials:
Anything that will create the environment of a Mexican plaza. Have a fiesta!

Directions:
There are many resources that can be found in a school environment that can help to create a room full of beautiful, and creative art and cultural centers in the room. Library books with bright covers can be displayed, for example, in the book corner.

Ask the children if they have something from Mexico in their homes. Perhaps there are families from Mexico who would be willing to lend your room some cultural items. The children would love to share their heritage!

With time, you can turn your room into a plaza by drawing murals on large pieces of butcher paper and hanging them on the walls. Tile roofs can be made from Quaker Oat boxes. (Cut the boxes in half and paint them red and make a roof for a refrigerator box decorated as an adobe house [casa]).

Buildings could be drawn on the chalkboard with colored chalk.

Have a fiesta day and set up all the art activities you have done and invite other classes in to see your art exhibit and serve them buñuelos and atole. (See recipes in Comida.) Be sure to decorate your room with piñatas, banners, etc. The children should dress in their serapes, rebozos, sombreros.

octubre

OCTOBER

día de los muertos

DAY OF THE DEAD

octubre (October) Contents

October English/Spanish Vocabulary

autumn	el otoño
bag	la bolsa
bag of candy	la bolsa de dulces
bat	el murciélago
black cat	el gato negro
broom	la escoba
candy	los dulces
It is cloudy	Está nublado
clown	el payaso
It is cold (weather)	hace frío
It is cool	hace fresco
costume	disfraz, traje
ghost	la fantasma
Halloween	Halloween
I'm afraid	tengo miedo
leaves	las hojas
mask	la máscara
prince	el príncipe
princess	la princesa
pumpkin	la calabaza
skeleton	el esqueleto
It is sunny	hace sol
trick or treat	los trick or treat
It is warm	hace calor
It is windy	hace viento
witch	la bruja

Nadie muere de la muerte . . .
todos morimos de la vida. Octavio Paz

Day of All the Saints (November 1)
and
Day of All the Dead (November 2)

El Día de Todos Los Santos and El Día de Todos Los Muertos are two important holidays in Mexico. Originally religious celebrations, they are now characterized by many secular traditions as well. During the middle of October, many Mexican families prepare to celebrate the reunion of the living with the non-living. It is a time to commemorate one's ancestors and, for "los muertos," a time to return home to make sure all is well and that they have not been forgotten. Banners of cut paper are strung outside, skeletal images appear in windows, and special sweets and toys are prepared for the children.

Mexican families usually celebrate All Saints' Day by attending church services. On the Day of the Dead they may also attend memorial services and visit the graves of ancestors, placing a wreath or altar there as a remembrance. Offerings of food, candles, and flowers may also be made as a way of showing respect.

The celebration is particularly delightful for children because of the strong sense of love and family as it is expressed through toys and treats. Masks, puppets, and tiny dolls are all part of the fun. A sweet favorite is the "calaveras de azúcar" or sugar skulls sometimes in bright colors or labeled with a child's name.

It is traditional for many families to attend the play *Don Juan Tenorio* by José Zorilla, which dramatizes the salvation of Don Juan's soul by his lover.

In Hispanic culture, The Day of the Dead is a celebration of life by combining a festive yet respectful celebration of death.

Vocabulario for
Day of All the Saints and Day of All the Dead

El Día de Todos Los Santos – A special day, November 1, to honor the saints.

El Día de Los Muertos – A day to remember one's ancestors by visiting their graves, preparing special foods and activities, and attending services. This day, November 2 is a day to celebrate life and death.

Calavera – A skull. Also a form of poetry written for the Day of the Dead.

Ofrenda – A raised place at which religious ceremonies may be performed, and a place to honor the dead.

Zempasúchitl – Marigold, a flower used to decorate altars on the Day of the Dead.

Don Juan Tenorio – A traditional play performed on the Day of the Dead.

Don Juan Tenorio

Don Juan Tenorio is a traditional melodrama performed in Mexico on the Day of the Dead. The play was written by José Zorilla y Moral in 1844. Don Juan was a character from the Spanish play "El Burlador de Sevilla" written by Tirso de Molnia in the seventeenth century.

The first scene opens in a tavern where Don Juan is known for his corruption. Don Juan has just won a bet in which he killed more people during a year than his friend, Don Luís.

In the second scene Don Juan kills the father of his girlfriend, Doña Inés finds out about her father's death, and she dies at Don Juan's feet. Don Juan then leaves the country.

Many years later Don Juan returns to find that his own father was killed for his son's crimes. His estate has been turned into a burial ground for his victims, and Don Juan enters the cemetery at night. The ghost of Doña Inés' father appears. He has come to avenge his daughter's death. Don Juan challenges him, but Death comes forward to take his soul to Hell. Doña Inés' soul intervenes, and both souls go to Heaven. Doña Inés' true love purified and conquered Don Juan Tenorio's soul.

Danza de los Viejitos
(Dance of the "Oldsters")

Dancers hobble to the dance area, single file, holding their backs and bending their knees, as if it hurts to walk.

Steps

Counts

2	Tap right heel on floor
2	Tap right toe on floor
2	Tap left heel on floor
2	Tap left toe on floor
Tap 3	Step right foot across left foot
Tap 3	Step left foot across right foot
Tap 5	Tap cane on floor
Hold 3	Twist head right
Hold 3	Twist head left
Hold 3	Twist trunk right
Hold 3	Twist trunk left
Tap 5	Tap cane on floor
Hold 3	Jump forward, feet together
Hold 3	Jump backward, feet together

Midway through the dance, "los viejitos" begin to leap and dance with energy and vitality. The dancers then resume the traditional steps and, when the dance is complete, hobble out as they entered.

Bag of Bones

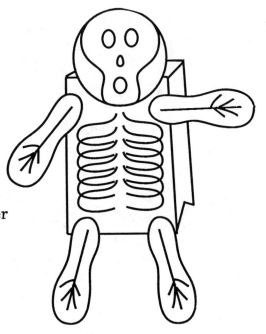

Materials:

    black felt-tipped pen

    6 inch paper plates

    white lunch bags

    1 sheet of white construction paper

    scissors

    paste

    string

Instructions:

1. Draw skull on a paper plate.

2. Draw skeletal torso on front and back of bag.

3. Cut out "light bulb" shapes from construction paper for arms and legs.

4. Draw arm and leg bones.

5. Paste head, arms and legs to bag as shown in illustration.

Place your "Bag of Bones" on the ofrenda, or hang them around the room.

String and Yarn Skulls

Materials:

9 x 12 piece of tag board

light colored pencil

white glue

1/8 inch yarn (white or pastel colors)

Begin yarn painting in the center and work outward. Place strands as close together as possible.

Instructions:

1. Draw skull design on tagboard (include space for a border).

2. Cut yarn into workable lengths.

3. Squeeze thin trail of glue into the center of the design, and let dry 2 minutes.

4. Press the yarn onto the glue with your thumbnail. Twist the end of the yarn to begin or end a length.

5. Fill in all of the spaces, and let it dry completely.

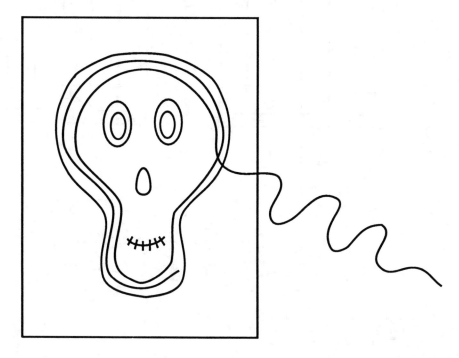

Coffin

Materials:
6 1/2" x 6" sheet of black tagboard or construction paper ruler, light-colored pencil, scissors, white poster paper, paint brush, cellophane tape, paste

Directions:
1. Divide the paper into six equal parts using the ruler and light-colored pencil.

2. Rule off one inch at each end (6" end) of paper.

3. Cut the tabs as shown by the dotted lines.

4. Decorate the coffin and let it dry.

5. Fold the paper on each ruled line overlapping sections A and F. Secure with cellophane tape where marked.

6. Tuck and paste tabs F to C, D to B, and E to A.

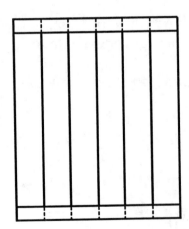 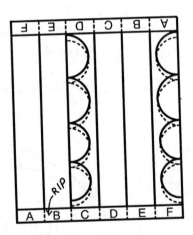

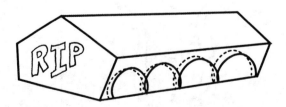

From *INDO HISPANIC FOLK ART TRADITIONS II/TRADICIONES ARTE SANALES INDO-HISPANASII* by Bobbi Salinas-Norman. Copyright © 1988. Piñata Publications, Oakland, California. Reprinted with permission.

Skull Mask

Materials:
    9" paper plate, pencil, scissors, sheet of white paper, black felt-tipped pen, glue, hole punch and two lengths of string at least 18" long.

Directions:
1. Hold the paper plate in front of the other person's face and mark, with the pencil, where the eyes and nose are.

2. Cut the eyes and nose holes in the paper plate and outline them heavily with the black felt-tipped pen.

3. Cut one 1 1/2 x 4" strip of white paper and draw teeth on it, leaving 1/2" blank and each side for tabs.

4. Glue both ends or tabs onto the plate so that the teeth protrude.

5. Punch holes on both sides of the plate and tie the strings through the holes.

Tin Toys

Materials:

disposable aluminum baking sheets, black felt-tipped pen, pointed instrument such as a ball point pen, scissors, enamel paints, 26 gauge fine wire

* Caution: The aluminum can be sharp so be careful!

Directions:

1. Draw the toy shape on the aluminum.

2. Cut out the shapes with scissors.

3. The details can be pressed in with the help of a pointed instrument.

4. Make a hole for hanging the toy and string it with the wire.

5. Paint them with the enamel paint. You will probably need two coats.

6. You can make a skeleton with the aluminum and connect the bones with the wire.

7. Christmas ornaments can be made with the aluminum at Christmas time.

From *INDO HISPANIC FOLK ART TRADITIONS II/TRADICIONES ARTE SANALES INDO-HISPANASII* by Bobbi Salinas-Norman. Copyright © 1988. Piñata Publications, Oakland, California. Reprinted with permission.

Skeleton "Paper Doll"

Materials:
   gold or pink tissue paper, strip cutout patterns, scissors

Directions:

1. Fold the paper into thirds lengthwise.

2. Cut three strips along the fold lines.

3. Place one strip on a flat surface.

4. Fold the strip so that the bottom meets the top edge. Crease with the thumb nail to make a sharp edge.

5. Make the same fold two more times.

6. Turn the paper so that the narrow way faces you. Using a pattern that you have provided, draw half a skeleton or skull with the center along the folded side.

7. Keep the paper folded and cut out the shape. Be sure to leave part of the right and left edges uncut so that the pattern will be continuous.

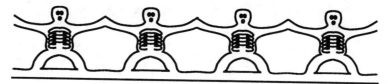

String these around your room or on your desk. The real ones are used in Mexico to decorate an "ofrenda." This technique can be used for other holiday that you might celebrate in the classroom — shamrocks, hearts, angels, Christmas trees etc.

From *INDO HISPANIC FOLK ART TRADITIONS II / TRADICIONES ARTE SANALES INDO-HISPANASII* by Bobbi Salinas-Norman. Copyright © 1988. Piñata Publications, Oakland, California. Reprinted with permission.

Plaster of Paris Mask

Materials:
>   approximately 40 to 50 pre-cut strips of plaster of paris gauze (available at art supply stores), 24" x 29" trash bag, petroleum jelly, 2 cups water in a bowl, sharp instrument, 2 lengths of 18" string, black felt-tip markers and pens, tempera paint and paint brushes (optional)

Directions:
1. Cut a hole in the bottom (sealed end) of a trash bag large enough to go over the child's head to keep the child's clothes clean while the plaster is being applied. It can be reused.

2. Apply a liberal amount of petroleum jelly to the parts of the student's face that will be covered with the plaster. (It might be helpful to have clips available to hold the children's hair back away from their face.)

3. Dip each strip of plaster into a bowl of water for a few seconds, then apply to the face. If making a full mask, it will be necessary to cover the area just below the jaw and chin line. **DO NOT COVER THE NOSTRILS OR THE MOUTH.**

4. The child should remain still until the plaster is firm enough to retain its shape when it is taken off.

5. Wipe the petroleum jelly off before washing the faces.

6. When the mask is completely dry, punch a hole in each side and tie a string through the holes.

* With very little children, it is best to cut the plaster strips into diamonds or triangles because of the small faces.

From *INDO HISPANIC FOLK ART TRADITIONS II / TRADICIONES ARTE SANALES INDO-HISPANASII* by Bobbi Salinas-Norman. Copyright © 1988. Piñata Publications, Oakland, California. Reprinted with permission.

Styrofoam Skeletons

Materials:
white chalk or crayon, 9" x 12" construction paper (black) styrofoam popcorn or beads from packings, glue and black fine point felt-tipped pen

Directions:
1. Draw a white stick figure on the black construction paper.

2. Before gluing, plan your skeleton by laying the different styrofoam shapes on the chalk marks and carefully set aside.

3. Carefully draw the features of a skull on a bead-shaped kernel of styrofoam with the felt tipped pen.

4. Glue the styrofoam shapes onto the paper.

Dancing Skeleton

Materials:

    white duplicating paper (8 1/2" x 5 1/4") 1/2 sheets, duplicated skeleton, black felt-tipped marker, scissors and glue

Directions:

1. Outline the skeleton with the black pen.

2. Cut out the skeleton.

3. On one side of the white paper, glue the tabs of the skeleton so that the skeleton protrudes or bends.

4. Hold up the paper, with the skeleton on the back to the light and move the paper slightly to the left and to the right and you will see the skeleton dance.

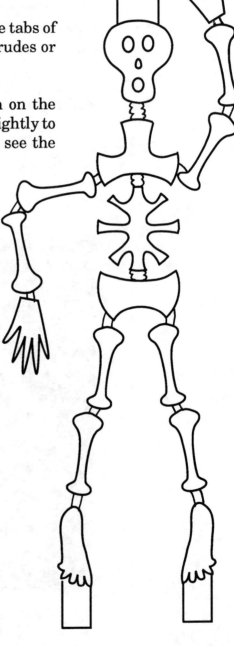

Mr. Potato Skull Prints

Materials:
- potato
- paper towels
- pencil
- sharp knife
- sponge
- tempera paint
- art or construction paper

Instructions:

1. Wash potato and dry with paper towels.

2. Cut potato in half to make a flat surface.

3. Mark skull design on potato with the pencil.

4. Use the knife to cut away eyes, nose, mouth, etc.

5. Soak sponge with paint.

6. Press potato into the sponge, then onto the paper to make prints.

Decorate the skull prints with foil, or write your name in glitter on the forehead to add a special touch.

Finger and Thumbprints

Materials:
    black or white tempera paint
    paper plate
    black or white construction paper
    black, white, and pastel felt pens

Instructions:
1. Put a small amount of paint on the plate.

2. Press thumb into the paint to cover completely.

3. Press onto paper, rock backward, then lift.

4. Draw the details in with the felt pens, when the prints are dry.

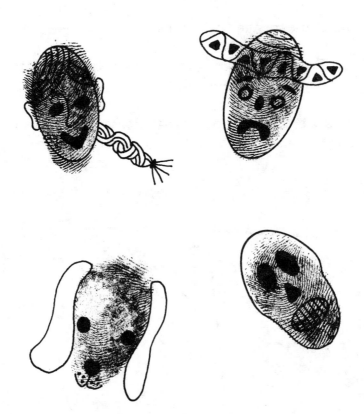

Atole de Leche

Ingredients:

2	cups water
1/2	cup "masa," finely ground white corn meal
1	inch cinnamon stick
4	cups milk
1	cup sugar

Cooking Instructions:

1. Blend corn meal and water.

2. Add cinnamon stick and boil mixture for about 10 minutes.

3. Add milk and sugar; bring to a boil, stirring constantly.

4. Remove cinnamon stick and serve hot.

Serves 8-10

Pan de Muertos

Ingredients:

2	cups bisquick
2	Tbsp. sugar
1	egg
2/3	cup water or milk
10	drops of anise extract

Cooking Instructions:

Heat oven to 400°.

Grease a large cookie sheet.

1. Mix all ingredients, and beat vigorously for 1/2 minute.

2. Give a small amount to each child and have them mold their own crossbones or skulls.

3. Sprinkle with topping.* See below.

4. Bake 20-25 minutes.

5. Serve warm with milk.

* Topping:
Combine 1/4 cup brown sugar, 1 Tbsp. flour,
1 tsp. cinnamon, 1 Tbsp. melted butter.

noviembre

NOVEMBER

la Virgen de Guadalupe

LADY OF GUADALUPE

noviembre (November) Contents

November English/Spanish Vocabulary

cactus	los nopales
candles	las velas
church	La Basílica
church	la iglesia
to eat breakfast	desayunar
to eat dinner	cenar
to eat lunch	almorzar
flowers	las flores
I eat breakfast at 6:00 A.M.	Desayuno a las seis de la mañana
I eat dinner at 6:00 P.M.	Ceno a las seis de la tarde
I eat lunch at noon	Almuerzo al mediodía
Lady of Guadalupe	La Virgen de Guadalupe
lady	doña
lady (married)	señora
lady (single)	señorita
leaves	las hojas
miracle	el milagro
Poncho, shawl	tilma
printing	imprimir (to print)
Thanksgiving	Día de gracias
turkey	el pavo, el guajolote

Legend of Our Lady of Guadalupe
or
La Virgen de Guadalupe

Once, many years ago there lived in the country of Mexico, an Indian named Juan Diego. His name had not always been Juan Diego for he and his wife had been converted by the Spanish monks and given a European name at his baptism. Both Juan and his wife, María Lucía were very devout in their belief in the new Christian faith they had acquired.

One winter, María became very ill and she died; however, the monks assured Juan that his wife, a good woman, was saved by their Father.

Juan continued to work hard and to live the same good life that he had lived with his wife. That is why every Saturday he would walk a long distance to go to the church in Santiago to pray for and to participate in a special mass for Mary, the Mother of God.

It was on a Saturday, the 9th of December, that Juan was making the long trip on foot to Santiago that the miracle of the Virgin of Guadalupe occurred.

As Juan Diego was on his way, he crossed the hill of Tepeyac and he heard heavenly music that sounded like a chorus of birds. Unbelieving, he stopped to listen.

"Juan – Juan Diego," a voice called.

Juan looked around and he saw a cloud and out of the cloud he saw a vision of the Holy Virgin appear before him. As he stared in awe he saw that she was dark-skinned and dressed in a flowing blue robe adorned with gold stars.

"Juan Diego," said the Lady, "the most loved and smallest of my children. Where are you going?"

Juan answered softly, "I am going to the Church of Santiago to celebrate the mass in honor of the Mother of God."

"My beloved son," she replied, "I am the Virgin Mary and I have chosen you, an Aztec, to go to the Bishop and ask him to build a church, on this spot, so I can show my love for all my children and especially the Indians."

Juan promised that he would convey the message and he ran to the house of the Bishop and nervously told of his day, his encounter and the wish of the Virgin Mary for a church in her honor. The Bishop and people with him laughed at Juan and would not listen to or would they believe what he had to say.

Juan returned to the hill at Tepeyac and there was the Virgin waiting for him. "I have failed," cried Juan. "They laughed at me and would not listen to what I had to say. Choose someone else other than a poor Indian."

"No, my son," she replied with a voice full of love. "I have chosen you. You must go back and try again."

The next day, which was Sunday, Juan went to Mass and with greater calm and reassurance, he made an appointment to see the Bishop and with a rehearsed speech, he carefully explained and described what had taken place and the request of the Virgin.

The Bishop listened and was very interested in what Juan had to say. The Bishop stated that if Juan could come back to him with some miraculous sign of the Blessed Virgin, then he would consider the request seriously.

Disappointed and depressed, Juan again returned to the hill at Tepeyac. What he did not know was that the Bishop had sent two members of his staff to follow him. What happened only served to strengthen Juan Diego's story for when he reached the spot where the Virgin was, he disappeared in the eyes of the followers.

Sadly, Juan explained the demands of the Bishop for some sign to show the truth in his story. The Virgin asked him to return the next day and she would have the sign that would be necessary to prove her existence.

Monday was a very dark day for Juan as his uncle, his only close relative fell gravely ill with a very high fever. The doctor did not hold much hope for his uncle's recovery so Juan readied himself to make the trip to the church to ask a priest to come to give his uncle the Last Rites. Juan began the trip but felt that he should go around the hill at Tepeyac for he was afraid to face the Virgin because he did not have the time to go to the church for Her.

As Juan wound his way through the cactus, he heard and saw the Virgin in front of him.

"Juan," she said, "don't worry. I know how hard this is for you and I know that your uncle is very ill. Your uncle will be fine. He is well now. Now, take my sign to the Bishop! It is ready for you. Go to the top of the hill and there you will find roses blooming among the cactus. Take them to the bishop."

When Juan reached the top of the hill, there were beautiful Castillian roses blooming.

"Carry them in your blanket," she instructed. "Use your tilma to carry them as if you were carrying corn. I will tell you what you have to say and do."

"This is the sign that the Bishop wants," continued the Virgin. "Do not show them to anyone except the Bishop. When he sees this, he will build the cathedral I have asked for."

At the Bishop's house, the guards refused to allow Juan Diego to enter until he had shown them what was in his tilma. Reluctantly Juan opened the tilma a little to show the roses but when the guards reached for the roses, they seemed to elude their grasp and became a part of the fabric.

Juan was allowed to enter and see the Bishop and Juan fully opened the tilma to drop the roses but when he did, everyone stood in awe and fell immediately to their knees. When Juan looked at his tilma, there emblazoned on the fabric was the image of the Virgin of Guadalupe with her brown skin and beautiful blue robe covered with gold stars.

The tilma was placed over the altar for all to worship and the church was built for the Virgin of Guadalupe. Many years later, another church was built next to the existing church at the foot of the hill at Tepeyac. Both cathedrals can be seen today on the outskirts of Mexico City.

The Virgin of Guadalupe is the Patron Saint of Mexico and many miracles have been attributed to her. It was said that a severe epidemic was stopped in 1544 when the tilma of Juan Diego was brought into the city.

Another miracle occurred when the Virgin caused the flood waters to subside in 1629.

A well, which opened under her feet during one of her appearances is said to have miraculous curing powers and is housed in the Chapel of the Little Well.

The image of the Virgin was even carried into battle for on September 16, 1810, the famous patriot Father Miguel Hidalgo y Costilla issued the "Grito de Dolores," which began the Revolution for Mexican Independence. The banner of Our Lady of Guadalupe was his standard and the battle cry rang out: "¡Viva La

Virgin de Guadalupe y muera el mal gobierno!" (Long live the Virgin of Guadalupe and down with bad government!" The Virgin became a symbol of strength and faith.

Over the years, endless processions of pilgrims crawled on their knees, their arms outstretched to form the cross or saying their rosaries, to the Shrine of the Virgin of Guadalupe, the holiest place in all Mexico. The tilma is housed here at the Basilica. No modern chemical laboratory has been able to analyze the composition of the pigment of the unfading colors of the tilma.

On December 12, 1931, the annual fiesta celebrated the four hundredth anniversary of the appearance of the apparition of the Virgin.

Las Flores/The Flowers

The flower plays a very important part in the lives and cultures in Mexico. The Mexican's love of color and pageantry in addition to the importance of tradition, make the flower a natural part of their existence.

The marigold (caléndula, maravilla, zempasúchitl) is always used on the altar or in the celebration of "El Día de los Muertos" (The Day of the Dead). It is the flower of eternity and a special part in remembering the loved ones who have died.

The red rose is another flower of importance as it was the red rose that convinced the Bishop to build a church for "La Virgen de Guadalupe." La rosa roja (red rose) was a sign given to Juan Diego to take to the Obispo (Bishop) by The Virgen as it was the wrong season for the roses to bloom and it was, therefore, a miracle.

On El Día de las Madres (Mother's Day), the flower again plays an important part in the celebrations. People whose mother is alive, wear red flowers and those whose mother is dead, wear white flowers.

Las Bodas and La Quinceñera are two more events that use flowers extensively. The wedding and the fifteenth birthday celebration for the girls use many white flowers. The fifteen year old girl is ushered through boughs of flowers that are held as arches by her friends as she celebrates her entrance into womanhood.

These are but a few ways that the flower is part of the traditions of Mexico. The color and beauty are a natural way for the Mexican to express himself and to lend another part to the fullness and celebrations so vital to the culture.

Paper Flowers

Crepe Paper Flowers

1. Cut strips of brightly colored crepe paper strips approximately 3" wide and 18" long.

2. Stretch the sides of crepe paper to make "ruffles."

3. Gather or pleat the strip in the center.

   Twist a pipe cleaner tightly around the center.

4. Pull the paper out to shape the flower gently not to stretch the paper.

Tissue Paper Flowers

1. Cut 5 squares of tissue paper 5" x 5".

2. Put all the squares, one on top of the other, in a pile.

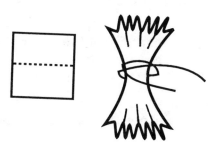

3. Gather the papers together in the center in a pleating manner. Tie the center with a pipe cleaner or tie for plastic bags.

4. At this point, it is possible to trim the edges by rounding them or cutting them in a zig-zag manner.

5. Holding the pipe cleaners, fan the paper to make the petals.

Paper Flowers

Coffee Filter Flowers

1. Use food coloring. Add several of drops to water in cups to make really bright colors. Use one cup for each color.

2. Fold each coffee filter three times to make a wedge shape.

3. Dip rounded edges in one color of dye and the pointed edge into another color.

4. Carefully open the filter and put it on newspaper to dry.

5. When completely dry, stack one, two or three dyed filters, crumbled together in the center to make a flower and staple it making sure to go through all the layers.

6. Tape the stapled center. It is possible to add a pipe cleaner stem.

Leaves for Coffee Filter Flowers

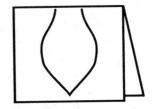

1. Cut a leaf from a folded piece of green crepe paper.

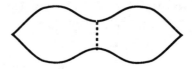

2. Open leaf but do not cut it at the fold.

3. Gather the leaf at the center and add it to the base of the flower.

Candles

The pilgrims, when they came to worship the Virgin de Guadalupe, often carried lighted candles.

Directions:

1. Place the paraffin in top of a double boiler (add crayon scraps if you want for color) along with water in the bottom, and put it on a heating unit.

2. Put a pencil in the center of a mold (a jello mold will be fine as long as it is heat resistant and will not melt with the heat of the paraffin).

3. While holding the pencil, pour the melted wax into the mold. You will have to hold the pencil until the wax begins to harden.

4. When the wax is hard, remove the pencil. Put a wick in the hole around the string.

5. Remove the wax from the mold by dipping it into hot water.

OR

Images/Printing

When Juan Diego arrived at the Bishop's house and he opened his "tilma," there, to everyone's astonishment was the picture of the Virgin, imprinted.

Printing Techniques and Ideas:

Potato Prints

1. Cut a potato in half.

2. Mark and cut around a simple shape on the flat side of the potato.

3. Pour a little paint in a shallow pan.

4. Dip the potato print into the paint and print. Make wrapping paper, greeting cards, etc.

Image I

1. Fold the desired paper in half down the middle.

2. Drip drops of paint on one side of the paper and re-fold the paper to make a print exactly like it on the other side.

3. Repeat if desired with different colors.

4. When done, open the paper and flatten to dry.

Image II

1. Use the same technique for "Image I" except make lines or a specific design to duplicate.

2. It is possible with this technique to write your name in cursive, close to the center line using it as a guide. In a bold color, write your name, fold the paper and you have a unique and different design.

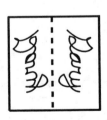

Art Prints

Materials:
1. styrofoam meat trays with smooth bottoms
2. cookie cutters
3. waterbase linoleum block ink
4. small art roller (brayer)
5. tissue paper or typing paper

Directions:
1. Make a design on the bottom of the meat tray with cookie cutters. Be careful not to push all the way through.

2. Put a little ink in another meat tray.

3. Rub the brayer in the ink until the roller is covered.

4. Roll the brayer over the design, place a piece of paper over the inked design, and you will have a print!

   Children may also draw a design with a dull pencil in the tray.

   Bev Bos – permission

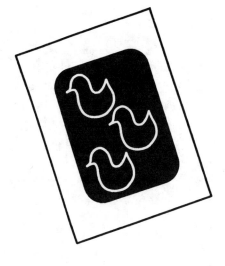

Cactus

When Juan Diego saw the Virgin, she asked him to go to the Bishop. As a sign, the virgin created a magnificent rose garden among the cactus.

There are over 1,000 kinds of cactus in Mexico! They are found in all sizes and shapes. Nearly all of them have very sharp spines called "espinas" in Spanish. They are succulents which means that they can go a long time without water because their thick skins and stems keep the water in the plant from evaporating. The "espinas" protect the plant from the desert animals. The spines have been used for needles, the "nopales" are used for food and the liquid is used for a beverage like alcohol.

1. From a 9" x 6" piece of green construction paper, cut a rounded shape.

2. With a black crayon draw the "espinas" and then cut out the cactus.

3. Accordion pleat the paper and put it inside a styrofoam or paper cup. Crumple and put paper of any kind around the cactus to hold it in the cup.

4. Cut 1" x 1" squares of brightly colored tissue paper.

5. Make cactus flowers by pinching small circles around the end of a pencil and paste them onto the cactus.

6. Decorate the cup with yarn painting (Chapter on March).

The Turkey – Mexico's Gift

Turkeys were known in Meso-America long before the Pilgrims landed at Plymouth Rock. Ocellated turkeys were native to the mountains of Southern Mexico from Michoacan to Oaxaca.

When Hernán Cortés landed in New Spain, he was so taken by the turkeys wandering around the pyramids of the Aztecs, that he sent one back to the King of Spain that year.

Turkeys can be made from apples, raisins, stuffed pimento olives and colored toothpicks.

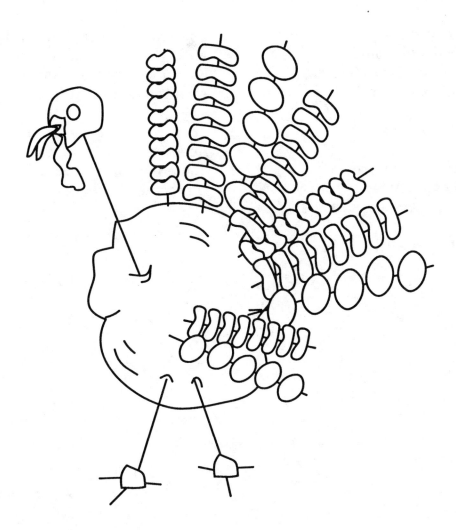

November Poems

Nopal Mexicano

Nopal Mexicano
de fuertes colores,
me gustan tus flores
blancas en ocasiones

Nopal de mi tierra
tus frutos son rojos
y son tus colores
los de mi bandera

Tú formas parte
de pabellón nacional
pues en tus fuertes pencas
se posó una águila real.

También formas parte
de bello paisaje
y se puede admirarte
en llanos y montes
y en el seco paraje.

¡Nopal Mexicano!

Cactus of My Land

Cactus of my land,
Your colors are so bright,
I love to see your cactus flowers
So beautiful and white.

Cactus of my land,
Your fruit is ruby red.
Your colors are like the flag
That flies above my head

You are a symbol of the nation
And grace my country's crest,
For on your noble branches
An eagle came to rest.

I find you in the mountains
And in the desert sand.
You are a noble citizen,
Oh cactus of my land!

Cooking with Nopales

Nopales can be purchased in jars in the Mexican or import section of your supermarket.

Nopales and Pork

Ingredients:

1 onion   4 pork steaks, or 1 1/2 lbs. lean pork
1 jar nopalitos   1 small can tomato sauce
soy sauce to taste   cooking oil

Cooking Directions:
Sauté onion until soft in cooking oil. Remove from pan and set aside. Cook pork into bite sized pieces sauté until lightly browned. Add 1 tsp. soy sauce (or more if you like a tangy flavor), the drained nopalitos, tomato sauce, onion and simmer 20 minutes.
Serve with rice. Serves 4.

Pickled Nopalitos

Ingredients:
1 jar nopalitos, drained   3/4 cup rice vinegar
1/3 cup sliced onion   1/3 cup sugar
cherry tomatoes
2 Tbsp. cilantro
1 tsp. cumin seed

Cooking Directions:
Pack nopalitos, tomatoes, onions, cumin, and cilantro in a pint jar. Combine sugar and vinegar in a saucepan and bring to a boil. Cook until sugar dissolves. Pour over nopales. Cover with lid, chill until next day. Keeps up to 2 weeks in the refrigerator.

Nopalitos and Eggs
Rinsed, drained and chopped nopalitos make a great addition to omelets or scrambled eggs!

diciembre

DECEMBER

las posadas

(LOOKING FOR THE INN)

diciembre (December) Contents

December English/Spanish Vocabulary

angel	el ángel
baby	el niño
barn	el granero
camel	el camello
cat	el gato
chicken hutch	el gallinero
chickens	las gallinas
Christmas	La navidad
Christmas Eve	La Nochebuena
Christmas gift	aguinaldo
corral	corral
cow	la vaca
Day of the King (wisemen)	El Día de los Reyes Magos
decorations	la decoración (las decoraciones)
dog	el perro
donkey	el burro
goat	la cabra
holidays	días feriados
horse	el caballo
Baby Jesus	El niño Jesús
kings	los reyes
lantern	la lámpara, la linterna
mice	los ratones
music	la música
New Years Eve	La nochevieja
ornaments	los ornamentos, los adornos
pig	el puerco
presents	los regalos
Santa Claus	Santa Claus
sheep	oveja
shepherd	el pastor (pastores)
stable	el establo
star	la estrella
turkey	el pavo, el guajolote
pinata	piñata

Las Posadas
(Looking for the Inn)

Every Christmas season, Mexican families celebrate "Las Posadas" to recreate the journey of Mary and Joseph as they search for lodging in Bethlehem before Christ is born. The custom began around 1554 in a convent near Tenochtitlán when priest, Diego de Sória was granted permission from the Pope to celebrate nine Misas de Aguinaldo, Gift Masses, to mark the nine days it took for Mary and Joseph to find lodging, *posada* in Spanish. The masses are celebrated outside each night beginning on the 16th of December and continuing for nine days until the 24th.

Today the celebration begins with a procession led by people dressed as Joseph and Mary who are followed by "angels" and "shepherds" as they go from door to door. As they stop at each house they sing verses of the traditional *Letanía*. Because the procession begins after dark, people carry candles and lanterns to light their way. Finally, after stopping at several houses, the weary travellers are invited in to rest, enjoy a special meal, a piñata, and dancing.

The *Nacimiento*, Nativity Scene, is a very important tradition in Mexico. Every family provides some space in their home for a nativity display. The figures may be of any size and may even occupy an entire room. Collecting figures for the Nacimiento is never complete and additional pieces are added to the scene over the years. When the scene is set up on December 16, the wise men are placed far away, and the baby's crib is empty. After the "misa del gallo" (crows mass) at midnight Christmas Eve the baby is placed in the manger. It is then that the wisemen move closer each day until on January 6th, the "Day of the Kings," they reach the manger. After the Christmas season is over, on January 6, the Nacimiento is carefully packed away for another year with the angel placed on the very top of the box to protect the figures until the next year.

Mojo, a Spanish moss which grows in cypress trees in the mountains of Mexico, is a traditional decoration for the rooms or the Nacimiento. They gray-green plant is nourished by air, and is sold in bunches in the markets during December.

Vocabulario for Las Posadas

Aguinaldo – A small Christmas gift of money, fruit, or candy.

Buñuelo – Large, flaky pastry, sprinkled with cinnamon and sugar, served on Christmas Eve.

Chocolate – Chocolate milk drink, usually served hot and spiced with cinnamon.

Farolito – A small lantern lighted by a candle, used to light the Posadas procession.

¡Feliz Navidad! – Merry Christmas!

Flor de Noche Buena – The poinsettia, Flower of Christmas Eve.

Mojo – Spanish moss used to decorate the Nativity scenes.

Misa del Gallo – Midnight mass on December 24, literally mass of the rooster.

Nacimiento – Nativity scene.

Navidad – Christmas

Posadas – A reenactment for the nine consecutive nights of Joseph's and Mary's search for lodging.

Christmas Music

Pedia de la Posada (Asking for Lodging)

En_ nom - bre del cie_____ e - b

os_ pi - do_ po - sa_____ da

pu - es no pue - de an - dar_____

mi_ es - po - sa a - ma_____

da a_ qui no es me - son_____

si - gan a - de - lan_____

te_____ yo____ no pue - do

a - brir_____ no____ sea al - gun

tu - nan_____ te.

San José

SAN JOSÉ
En nombre del cielo
Os pido posada,
Pues no puede andar
Mi esposa amada.

CASERO
Aquí no es mesón;
Sigan adelante.
Yo no puedo abrir;
No sea algun tulante.

SAN JOSE
No seas inhumano;
Tenos caridad.
Que el Dios de los cielos
Te lo premiara.

CASERO
Ya se pueden ir
Y no molestar.
Porque si me enfado
Los voy a apalear.

SAN JOSE
Venimos rendidos
Desde Nazareth.
Yo soy carpintero
De nombre José.

CASERO
No me importa el nombre;
Déjenme dormir,
Pues que ya les digo
Que no hemos de abrir.

SAN JOSE
Posada te pido,
Amado casero,
Por sólo una noche,
La Reina del Cielo.

CASERO
Pues si es una reina
Quien lo solicita,
¿Cómo es que de noche
Anda tan solita?

St. Joseph

ST. JOSEPH
In the name of Heaven
I beg you for lodging,
For she cannot walk
My beloved wife.

MAN OF THE HOUSE
This is not an inn
So keep going;
I cannot open;
You may be bad people.

ST. JOSEPH
Don't be inhuman;
Have mercy on us.
The God of the heavens
Will reward you for it.

MAN OF THE HOUSE
Better go on
And don't bother us.
For if I become angry,
I shall beat you up.

ST. JOSEPH
We are worn out
Coming from Nazareth.
I'm a carpenter
My name is Joseph.

MAN OF THE HOUSE
Your name doesn't matter;
Let me sleep,
For I am telling you
We shall not open.

ST. JOSEPH
Lodging is asked of you
Dear man,
For just one night
By the Queen of Heaven.

MAN OF THE HOUSE
Well, if it's a queen
Who solicits it,
Why is it that at night
Does she travel so alone?

SAN JOSE

Mi esposa es Maria
Es Reina del cielo
Y madre va a ser
Del Divino Verbo.

CASERO

Eres tu Jose?
tu esposa es María?
Entren, perigrinos,
No los conocía.

SAN JOSE

Dios pague, señores,
Vuestra caridad,
Y así os colme el cielo
De felicidad.

CASERO

Dichosa la casa
Que abriga este día
A la Virgen Pura,
La Hermosa María.

SAN JOSE

Dichosa esta casa
Que nos da posada;
Dios siempre le de
Su dicha sagrada.

CASERO

Posada os damos
Con mucha alegría,
Entra, José justo,
Entra con María.

ST. JOSEPH

My wife is Mary
She's the Queen of Heaven
And she's going to be the mother
Of the Divine Word.

MAN OF THE HOUSE

Are you Joseph?
Your wife Mary?
Enter, pilgrims,
I did not know you.

ST. JOSEPH

May god pay, señores,
Your kindness,
And thus the Heavens heap
Happiness upon you.

MAN OF THE HOUSE

Fortunate the house
That shelters this day
The pure Virgin,
The beautiful Mary.

ST. JOSEPH

Fortunate this house
That gives us shelter;
May God always give it
Its sacred happiness.

MAN OF THE HOUSE

Lodging I give you
With much joy;
Enter, just Joseph,
Enter with Mary.

The following verses are sung by the groups inside the house and outside; however, once the doors are opened, they sing them together.

A - bran - se las puer - tas rom - pan - se los vo - los que vien a po - sar el Rey de los cie - los que viene a po - sar___ el Rey de los cie - los.

Abrense las puertas!
Rómpense los velos;
Que viene a posar
El Rey de los Cielos.

Entrad pues, esposos,
Con satisfacción,
Que os damos posada
Con el corazón.

Entren, santos perigrinos,
Reciban este rincón,
No de este pobre morada
Sino de mi corazón.

Esta noche es de alegría,
De gusto y de regozijo,
Porque hospedamos aquí
A la Madre de Dios Hijo.

Let the doors fly open!
Let the veils be broken!
For here comes to rest
The King of the Heavens.

Enter then spouses,
With satisfaction,
For we're giving you lodging
With our hearts.

Enter, holy pilgrims,
Receive this corner,
Not of this poor dwelling
But of my heart.

This night is of joy,
Of pleasure and rejoicing,
Because we are lodging here
The Mother of God, the Son.

Noche de Paz
(Silent Night)

Franz Gruber

No-che de paz, no-che de a-mor, To - do duer-me en
No-che de paz, no-che de a-mor, To - do duer-me en
No-che de paz, no-che de a-mor, To - do duer-me en

re - de - dor. Só - lo sue - nan en la os - cu - ri - dad
re - de - dor. So - bre el san - to ni ño Je - sús
re - de - dor. Fie - les, ve - lan a - llí en Be - lén

Ar - mo - ni - as de fe - li - ci - dad, Ar - mo - ní - as de
U - na es - tre - lla es - par - ce su luz, Bri - lla so - bre el
Los pas - to - res, la ma - dre tam - bien Y la es - tre - lla de

paz, Ar - mo - ní - as de paz.____
Rey, Bri - lla so - bre el Rey.____
paz, Y la es - tre - lla de paz.____

La Primera Navidad
The First Noel

Traditional

Na - vi - dad,___ Na - vi - dad! Qué___ dul - ce el
Na - vi - dad,___ Na - vi - dad! Na - ci - do es-

son De___ co - ros ce - les___ tes so - bre Be -
tá El___ ni - ño Je - sus,___ el Sal - va -

lén! Na - vi - dad,___ Na - vi - dad! Qué___ dul - ce el
dor Y___ so - bre Be - lén ra - dian - te es -

son A los bue - nos pas - to - res de Be - lén!
tá La es - tre - lla de___ di - vi - no ful - gor.

Na - vi - dad,___ Na - vi - dad, Na - vi -

dad, Na vi - dad,_____ Al nue - vo

Rey a - do - rad, a - do - rad.

Venid, Fieles Todos
O Come All Ye Faithful

Old Latin Hymn

Ve - nid, fie - les to - dos,
Ve - nid, fie - les to - dos,

A Be - lén mar - che - mos, Go - zo - sos, triun-
En Be - lén ve - re - mos Al ni - ño di-

fan - tes y lle - nos dea - mor.
vi - no, al ni - ño Je - sús.

Cris - to ha na - ci - do, Cris - to el Rey di-
Paz en la tie - rra Glo - ria en las al-

vi - no! Ve - nid,— a - do - re - mos, Ve-
tu - ras!

nid,— a - do - re - mos, Ve - nid,— a - do-

re - mos a nues - tro Se - ñor. A - mén.

Los Reyes de Oriente
We Three Kings

John H. Hopkins

Re - yes de O - rien - te son,
Re - yes de O - rien - te son
Bal - ta - zar, Gas - par y Mel - chor

Van en bus - ca de Je - sús;
Que ca - mi - nan ha - cia Be - lén;
Van en bus - ca de Je - sús

Por la tie - rra van gui - a - dos
Van a con - tem - plar el ros - tro
Lle - van do - nes de in - cien - so,

Por u tia - es - tre - lla.
Del di - vi - no Rey.
O - ro y mi - rra.

Oh be - lla es la san - ta luz,

la ma - ra - vi - llo - sa luz

Que los gui - a al pe - se - bre

Del di - vi - no Rey Je - sús.

Pueblecito de Belén
O Little Town of Bethlehem

Lewis H. Redner

Oh pueb - le - ci - to de Be - lén, La
Oh pueb - le - ci - to de Be - lén, La

cu - na de Je - sús, Ben - di - to pueb - lo
cu - na de nues - tro bien, Sa - gra - do pueb - lo

de Be - lén, La cu - na de Je - sús, El
de Be - lén, La cu - na de nues - tro bien, Ya

Rey tan a - do - ra - do, El san - to Re - den -
bli - lla en tus ca - lles Un be - llo res - plan -

tor; El Rey que vi - no al mun - do A
dor; Ya bri - lla en el mun - do La e -

dar - nos paz y a - mor.
ter - na luz de a - mor.

Molas

1.　Choose a pair of mola patterns and 3 pieces of paper the same size but of different colors (or wrapping paper).

2.　On tagboard, trace the patterns and cut out the shaded part. (Note: the teacher could by-pass this step by having the tracing forms ready ahead of time.)

3.　Trace patterns **B** and **C** on two different colors of paper and cut out the shaded part.

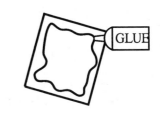

4.　Using the frame part, put glue around the edge of paper **A** (plain colored paper without a cut-out) and place frame **B** on top.

5.　Put glue around the edge of frame **B** and put frame **C** on top.

6.　In making your own patterns be sure you have a whole cut-out and a part of the whole.

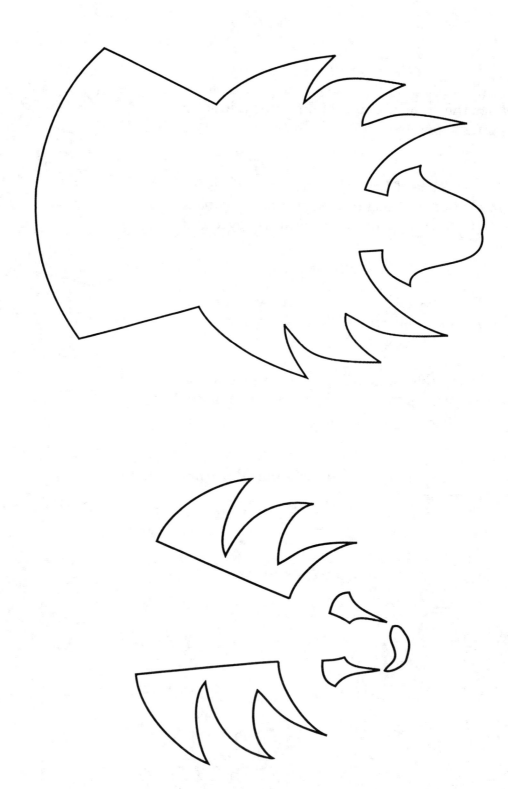

The angel protects and watches over the others. In packing away the Naciamento, the angel is always placed on top of the other figures to protect them until the next year.

Suggested colors: **A** white **B** red **C** green

Suggested colors:
A orange
B black
C yellow or contrasting color

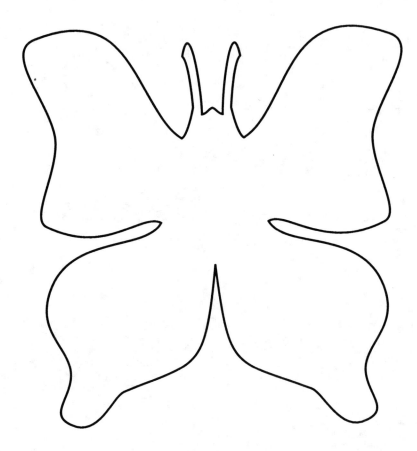

The butterfly is believed to contain the souls of the warriors killed in battle.

Pedro's Christmas Flower
Mexican Folk Tale

"How are you this morning, Mamá?" Pedro spoke softly as he bent over the thin white-faced woman who lay on the cot.

"Better maybe – a little better, Pedro," she whispered. "Perhaps I can get up soon – maybe mañana, Pedro."

But Pedro knew that it was not so. Each day his tired little mother grew thinner and paler. If only he could have a good doctor come to the little adobe hut. If only there was medicine for her. But medicine cost money and Pedro earned hardly enough for food from the sale of firewood.

Pedro sighed as he closed the door. Today he must buy beans and if there was enough money left, a small piece of meat. How he would like to buy a Christmas present for his mother! He would buy one of the silver necklaces which the silversmith sold. Or he'd buy a pair of silver earrings. But, alas, that could never be.

Pedro placed the saddle baskets on each side of the little brown burro and let him out of the shed. The sunshine was bright but the air was crisp.

He walked behind the donkey, switching his long stick gently over the animal's back. Now and then Pedro would stop to pick up a piece of dried mesquite or a piece of dead cactus. These he loaded into baskets. But wood was hard to find on the desert. He walked farther than he had ever gone before.

He climbed a little rise of ground and stood on the sandy knoll looking down into the little valley below. A tiny stream trickled from a small rocky cliff. It ran into a little pool. Beside the pool, growing close to the water were some tall pretty red flowers. Their leaves were a glossy green. They shone like the wax candles in the church. Pedro ran down the slope to the flowers.

"They're beautiful," he cried, "Like – like Christmas. I'll pick Mama a bouquet for a Christmas surprise." He bent and picked a beautiful bright red blossom. But almost as soon as he had pulled the stalk from its root, it withered. Its petals seemed to shiver and fade. The white sap dripped onto his fingers.

"Oh," Pedro cried," they bleed. They die! But perhaps if I dig the roots too, they will keep for Mama's Christmas." He took a sharp stick and dug carefully about the roots. Soon he had a soft ball of earth with the red flower standing proudly upright in the middle. Pedro put the plant in the corner of one of his wood baskets. Then he kept on gathering firewood. When the baskets were full, he turned the little burro back toward home, it was still early when he stopped at the house of his first customer.

"Buenos días," Señora Martínez greeted him. "What a lovely flower you have there, Pedro!"

"A beautiful flower," said a man who was standing beside the donkey. He was a stranger and had difficulty speaking the language.

"It is for my mamá," Pedro said. "It is for her Christmas."

"Dr. Poinsett is a great lover of flowers," Señora Martínez said. "At his home in the United States he has a greenhouse where he raises many flowers."

"But that one," the tall doctor said, "is a new one to me. It is very lovely. Would you sell it, boy?"

"It is for Mamá," Pedro said, Then quickly, "But if you are a doctor, perhaps you could help me, sir. My mama is very sick and there is no doctor. If you would come, sir, I could show you where these flowers grow. You could have all of them you want."

"You say your mother is ill?" The doctor had forgotten the flower.

"Oh, yes, and white and thin, I try to help her but she needs medicine."

"I will come," the doctor said. "One moment and I will be with you."

The good doctor got his black bag and Pedro led the way to the adobe hut. Pedro waited outside while the doctor made his examination. It seemed a long time before he came out, but Pedro was glad to see a smile on his face.

"Good food and the right medicine will cure her. You and I will go into the village and get what she needs. She is very sick now but she will get better soon."

"Oh, Dr. Poinsett," Pedro cried, "you mean she will be well and strong again?"

"Yes," said the doctor, "but she will need fruit and vegetables. Beans are not enough. Come, we will go shopping."

They went to the village and the good doctor bought fruit, vegetables, meat and milk. "You must eat these good foods too, Pedro," said the doctor. "I will bring some each day while I am staying with Señora Martinez. Then I will leave money for you to buy more good food."

"Gracias, gracias," cried Pedro. He prepared the food for dinner and hurried to wash and put away the dishes. Then he put the baskets on the burro and hurried away to the little valley. The sun was going down before he finished digging out the roots of a beautiful red flower like the one he had dug for his mother. He took it to the good doctor.

"Here is your Christmas flower," said Pedro.

"It will be the Christmas flower of many people," said the doctor, "just wait and we shall see."

"It shall be my poinsettia flower," said Pedro. "I shall name it for you. You are making my mother well and we shall have a good Christmas."

"Poinsettia is a good name," said the doctor. "We shall call it that."

So Pedro's red flower is now the Christmas flower, not only to one nation but to many. It is raised all over the country from which it came. Scarcely a cottage in Mexico is without its tall red flowers that almost cover the house at Christmas time. Pedro's flower is truly a great gift.

Pinwheel Poinsettia

1. Measure and cut one eight inch square of red construction paper.

2. Draw exact lines across the square, corner to corner. Add five black dots.

3. Cut dotted lines (approximately) 4" from the corners.

4. Fold the dotted corners to the center dot.

5. Using one brad, put the poinsettia together – center, pinwheel poinsettia and the three leaves on the bottom.

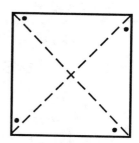

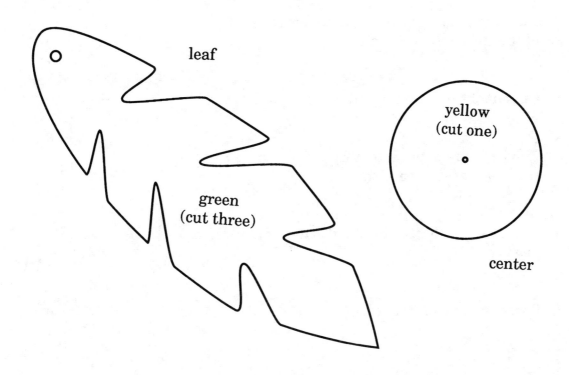

leaf

green
(cut three)

yellow
(cut one)

center

Tree of Life

The Tree of Life is part of the tradition of clay figures in Mexican art, for use on home altars. It may serve as a candleholder or simply as a decoration.

Materials:
    two large (dinner size) paper plates
    ruler
    pencil
    scissors
    8 1/2 x 11 inch drawing paper
    paste or glue
    felt pens

Directions:
1. Students draw figures of the Nativity scene which they would like to include in their Tree.

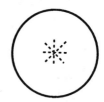

2. Divide the paper plates into 8 equal parts with the ruler and pencil.

3. Cut along the lines as shown to form the base of the tree.

4. Cut out the center of the other plate as shown.

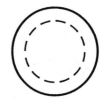

5. Roll drawing paper into a tube and secure in the base of the Tree with glue.

6. Decorate the base, ring, and tube with felt pens.

7. Paste the ring on the tube.

8. Paste the figures the children have drawn on the Tree.

Aguinaldos
(Little Gifts)

When the travelers in the Posadas procession finally arrive at their destination. The hostess of the house provides them with "aguinaldos," little gifts, as part of the party.

Materials

dinner plate (for tracing)
pencil
11" x 11" sheet of construction paper, any color
1 sheet of crepe paper
scissors
crayons or felt pens
cellophane tape
glue or paste
glitter
ribbon

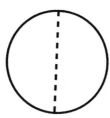    

Directions:

1. Trace around dinner plate to make circle on construction paper.

2. Cut out circle.

3. Fold in half, then cut on fold line, see illustration.

4. Draw decorations on both halves.

5. Roll one half-circle into a cone, overlap ends, and tape.

6. Repeat with the second half-circle.

7. Cut crepe paper into two 4" x 12" strips.

8. Glue crepe paper inside cone 1" down from top edge.

9. Let dry thoroughly, then fill with fruit, candy, coins or small toys. Tie the top with a ribbon.

10. Make a second aguinaldo with remaining cone.

Bread Dough Ornaments

Ingredients:
- 2 cups flour
- 2 cups salt
- 1 cup cornstarch
- 1 cup water
- food coloring (optional)

Materials:
- cookie cutters or dull knife
- wire
- scissors
- tempera paints
- clear spray
- glitter

Instructions:
1. Mix ingredients until dough is smooth like clay.

2. Roll out to 1/2 inch thickness on floured board.

3. Use cutters or knife to cut Christmas shapes.

4. Bend one short piece of wire and press both ends into the dough.

5. Let ornaments dry for a half hour.

6. Bake on foil covered cookie sheet in 200° oven until they begin to brown.

7. Let ornaments cool for an hour before decorating with paint or glitter.

Angel

Angels are Heaven's special messengers to Earth. During the Christmas season angelic images are found everywhere in Mexico.

Reproduce for each child. Children may color or paint, cut-out and add a photo of their own face. Hang or tape to walls to decorate classroom.

Tin Lantern

Hojaleteros, tin crafters, make masks, mirrors, candelabras, and many other items of tin. The tradition began centuries ago when gold and silver artisans were forbidden by the Spaniards to use precious metals. Today tin lanterns lighted by candles glow in the homes of Mexican families at Christmas time.

Materials:
    empty tin can with no sharp edges
    felt pen
    hammer
    nails of different sizes
    votive candle and holder
    small towel
    wire or pipe cleaner for hanging

Directions:

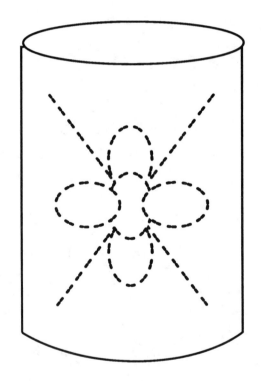

1. Draw dot design on the empty can.

2. Fill can with water up to 1/4 inch below the rim.

3. Freeze can for 2 days

4. Lay can of frozen water on folded towel & hammer holes following the dot design.

5. Hammer 2 holes on opposite sides, near rim for hanging wire.

6. Let ice melt, empty and dry can.

7. Light candle, drip a small amount into the bottom of the can, and secure candle holder there.

Luminarias

Fray Alonso Benavides wrote about the use of farolitos, little lanterns, by the Spanish colonists early in the 17th century. The original luminarias were huge stacks of kindling used as a bonfire on the roofs of adobe houses. The custom of using paper bags for luminarias began after World War I. Today luminarias are seen in New Mexico and Mexico at Christmas and other special occasions. Old timers may still refer to them as farolitos.

Materials:
    paper lunch bags
    sand
    1 votive candle and holder
    markers, paints, crayons
    scissors

Directions:
1. Bags can be cut or colored to decorate if desired.

2. Fold top edge of bag down.

3. Pour sand into the bag.

4. Place candle into the holder. Put the candle and holder in the sand in the bag.

Check with your local fire department regarding use of the luminarias to decorate your house or driveway.

Christmas Tree Piñata

Materials:
    1 large piece of tagboard
    stapler
    green crepe paper
    candy scissors
    assorted construction paper
    white glue

Directions:

1. Shape the tagboard into a cone and staple to hold. Leave a small opening at the top and cover the bottom with another piece of tag. Tape or staple to secure.

2. Make 1 inch wide strips of green crepe paper, gather and wrap around until all the tag is covered. You may need to use some white glue to secure it.

3. Make paper ornaments with construction paper. Decorate with glitter, crayon, etc. Hang on the ruffled edge of the crepe paper.

4. Fill up the piñata with candy and cover the top opening.

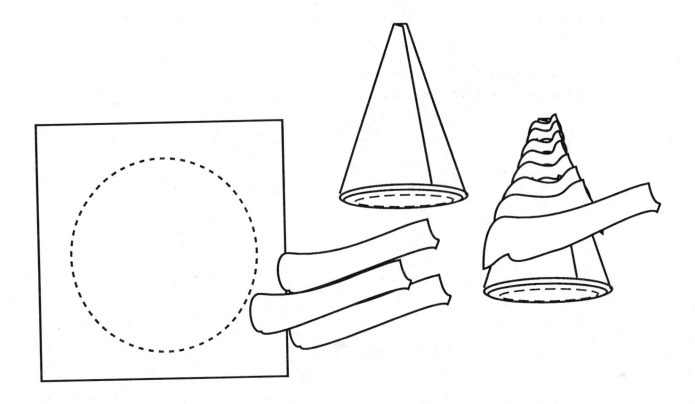

Buñuelos

Ingredients:
- 4 cups flour
- 2 Tbsp. lard
- 2 tsp. salt
- 1 tsp. baking powder
- 1 1/2 cups lukewarm water

Cooking Instructions:
1. Sift dry ingredients together.

2. Cut in lard, add water and knead until smooth. Let stand 20 minutes.

3. Divide the dough into 12 balls of uniform size.

4. Flatten each ball and stretch to a 5 inch diameter.

5. Deep fry at 425° until golden

6. Sprinkle with sugar and cinnamon and eat!

Fast Method:
Use 1 dozen flour tortillas

Chocolate Mexicano

Chocolate is a food native to America and a popular beverage in Mexico. The Mexicans make it from sweetened chocolate, spiced with cinnamon, and beat it until it foams with a little wooden mill called a molinillo.

Children in Mexico sing this little rhyme about chocolate when using the molinillo.

Chocolate
One, two, three, cho
One, two, three, co
One, two, three, la
One, two, three, te
Cho-co-late, cho-co-late
Beat, beat the cho-co-late.

Chocolate
Uno, dos, tres, cho
Uno, dos, tres, co
Uno, dos, tres, la
Uno, dos, tres, te
Cho-co-late, cho-co-late
Bate, bate, cho-co-late.

(Children rub hands together as if using the molinillo.)

Ingredients:
1/2 squares unsweetened chocolate
2 tsp. sugar
1/4 tsp. cinnamon
1 cup milk

Directions:
Heat all of the ingredients in a double boiler until the chocolate melts. Beat with an egg beater or pour in blender and blend until foamy. Yum!

Ensalada De Noche Buena
(Christmas Eve Salad)

This traditional Christmas Eve salad used to be served in Mexico with a sprinkling of sugar. Today it is often served with french dressing or mayonnaise.

Ingredients:
1 head lettuce, shredded
3 sliced cook beats
3 sliced red apples
3 slices pineapple, quartered
2 peeled oranges, sliced
2 bananas, sliced
1/2 cup roasted peanuts
1/2 cup pomegranate seeds

Directions:
1. Spread the lettuce on a large plate.

2. Arrange beets and fruits in a symmetrical pattern, alternating colors.

3. Sprinkle with nuts and pomegranate seeds.

4. Serve desired dressing separately.

   Serves 8

Churros

This sweet pastry originated in Spain, where it is often eaten for breakfast and at fairs and fiestas. The pastry is often enjoyed with a cup of chocolate for dipping.

Ingredients:

1 cup water
1/2 cup butter
1 cup flour
dash salt

3 or 4 eggs
oil or shortening for frying
powdered sugar

Directions:

Bring water to a boil in saucepan. Add butter. As soon as it is melted, dump in flour and salt. Stir over medium heat until it forms a single mass. Remove from heat, let cool slightly, then beat in the eggs one at a time. Put dough into pastry bag, and squeeze into hot oil in the shape of spirals. Oils should be about 375°. Fry until brown, drain, sprinkle with powdered sugar, and enjoy!

Empanadas
(Mexican Turnovers)

Empanadas are Mexican turnovers. They may be baked or fried and filled with meat, vegetables, fruit or sweets. Use any pie pastry, roll it thin and cut into 3" circles. Fill with a spoonful of the desired filling, moisten the edges of pastry with water, fold over, and press edges firmly with a fork. Deep fry at 400° until brown, or bake at 400° for 15 minutes, until brown. Dust with powdered sugar while still warm.

Here are some traditional fillings:
1. 1 cup crushed, drained pineapple mixed with 1/2 cup grated coconut.

2. 1 cup applesauce, mixed with 1/4 cup chopped nuts.

3. 1/2 cup mashed, cooked yams mixed with 1/2 cup coconut and 1/2 cup crushed pineapple.

4. 1 cup chopped raisins or dates, mixed with 1/2 cup chopped nuts. Bind together with a bit of jelly or syrup.

Sopapillas

These originated in New Mexico, which also celebrates Christmas in the Mexican tradition.

Ingredients:
 4 cups flour
 4 tsp. baking powder
 1 tsp. salt
 2 tsp. sugar
 3 Tbsp. lard or shortening
 water as needed, about 3/4 cup
 oil for cooking
 honey to taste

Cooking Instructions:
 1. Sift flour, baking powder, salt and sugar together.

 2. Cut in shortening, then add water to make a dry dough.

 3. Let dough stand 20 minutes.

 4. Roll out dough on lightly floured board to 1/4" thickness. Cut into 3" squares.

 5. Heat oil to 400°.

 6. Drop 1 square into oil, use fork to submerge. Flip over and fry until square puffs and browns. Remove and proceed with next square. Drain on paper towels.

 7. Cut one corner off each sopapilla and drizzle a little honey into it.

 Makes 4 dozen.

enero

JANUARY

THE LEGEND OF CHINA POBLANA

(costumes) (clothes)

enero (January) Contents

The Legend of China Poblana

One of the most-loved stories or legends of Mexico revolves around that of the China Poblana. It goes back to 1684 when the Mexican seas were infested with pirates. A Chinese boat was on its way from Manila to Acapulco when it was stopped by an English band of pirates. On the boat was a very beautiful Chinese princess named Mina and she was taken captive along with all her valuable cargo and possessions.

The chief of the pirates was not interested in her so he sold her in Manila to a merchant who was sailing to Acapulco. In Acapulco, he sold Mina to Captain Miguel Sousa as a slave. He took her to his city of Puebla where he was a respected and wealthy merchant.

Captain Sousa cared deeply for Mina and he gave her jewels and treasures and had her baptized. She was given the name of Catarina de San Juan, after a young nun who had just died, daughter of friends of the Sousas.

As time passed, Catarina was put under the care of Mother Superior and her Father Confessor for her education. She became a very devoted Christian and lived a very pure and simple life. She was said to have sold the pearls that Captain Sousa had given her to buy clothes for the poor children and the rest of her jewels she gave to the church.

Never again did she wear anything that wasn't the most simple and plain. Most of the time she was seen wearing a plain red flannel skirt, shirt and rebozo (sash). In the winter she wore a humble goatskin suit.

The beauty, physically and spiritually, of Catarina was so appealing and inspiring that all the other girls in the convent wanted to be exactly like Catarina and copied her dress complete with the red flannel skirt, white blouse and rebozo folded over their shoulders and crossed in front.

One Christmas night Catarina sat in the convent yard listening to the sounds and waiting to go to Mass. Out of the night, appeared The Virgin of the Sorrows.

"Catarina," said The Virgin, "You have given so selflessly to all the children and you have been so faithful and loyal to God, that I am going to give you a reward for your unselfishness. You will go to sleep now and wake up when the bells ring. You will find a reward in that you will be able to cure and also, you will see a sign that I have been here to be with you."

The bells rang and Catarina woke up. The Virgin had really been there for her skirt was no longer plain but it was embroidered with intricate designs in beads and sequins. The blouse was also embroidered.

Catarina's dress became the national costume for Mexico and it is worn by the girls and women on fiesta days and especially when dancing the Jarabe Tapatia (*The Mexican Hat Dance*).

The China Poblana costume has lasted throughout the centuries and Catarina's own dress is preserved in the State Museum in Puebla.

Not much is known about the later years in Catarina's life but it is told that when Catarina died, the church officials carried her coffin on their shoulders and the people throughout the state mourned the woman who had given so much of herself to the poor and the sick.

It is no wonder that the people when speaking about Catarina refer to her as China Poblana – the little Chinese woman of Puebla.

Note: It should be noted that there are many different legends of China Poblana with different facts and data but the important thread that runs throughout all the different accountings is the fact that Catarina was a person who cared greatly for the poor and the sick and contributed a lot in time and caring to these people.

National Costumes

Most of the clothing worn in Mexico today is the same as what is worn all over the United States; however, this is mainly true of the cities for in the country the dress is more simple. The men wear white cotton trousers (*pantalones*) and shirts (*camisas*). The sandals are called *huaraches* and a *serape* is often worn for warmth. The men also wear the wide-brimmed hat called the *sombrero*.

The women wear full skirts and blouses. You rarely see the women in the pueblos in pants. In the very small villages, the women and men may go barefoot.

Fiesta clothing is, however, different. The women of Tehuantepec wear a white, lacy headdress called a *huipil*. The legend says that many years ago a English ship was shipwrecked and many items washed on shore. Among those were baby clothes and the women thought they were to wear on the head and have continued to do so.

The *china poblana* dress is the national dress and is worn in the dance, "Jarabe Tapatia." The men in this dance wear the *charro* suit which consists of boots, tight pants, a *bolero* or short jacket, a colorful tie and a wide brimmed and beautifully decorated sombrero. The mariachi also wear this costume (band members – see music).

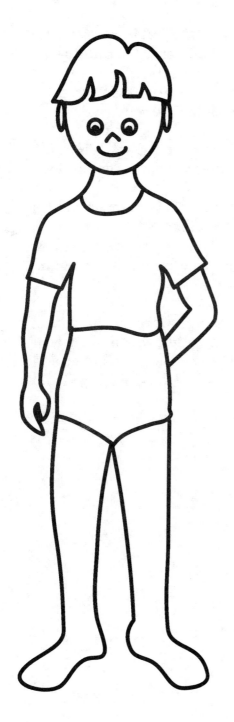

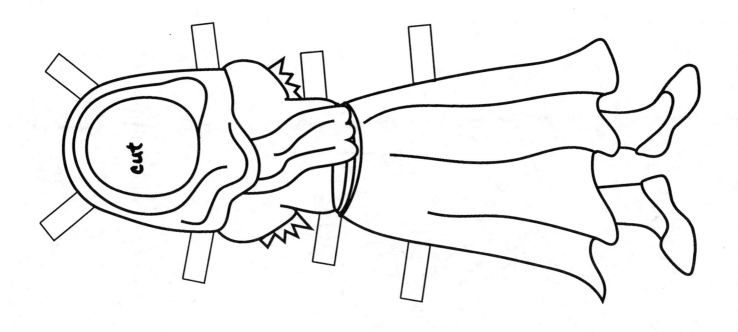

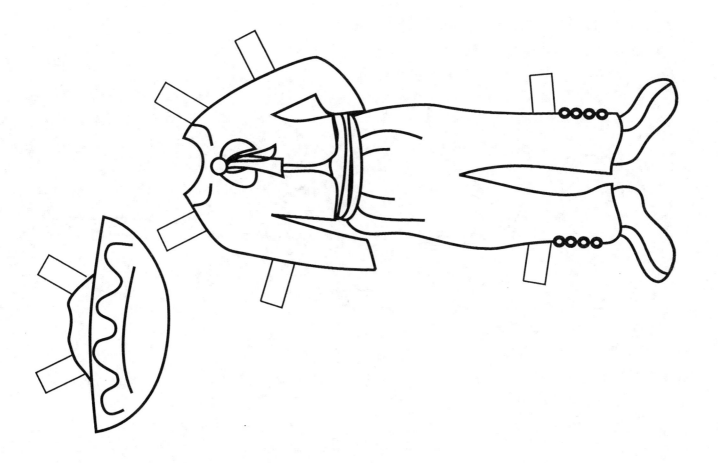

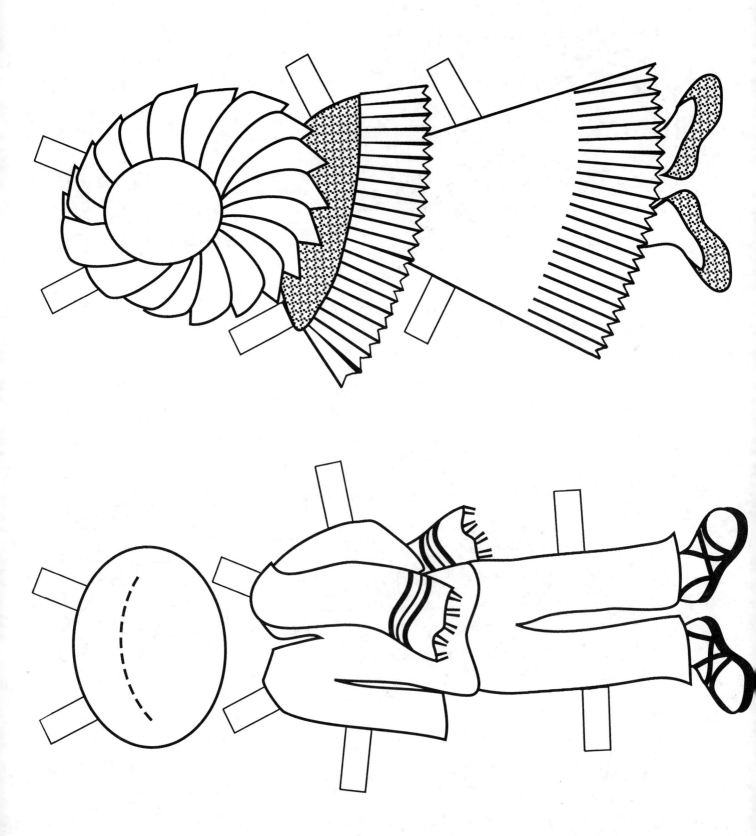

January English/Spanish Vocabulary

apron	delantal
belt	cinturón
blouse	blusa
boots	botas
bows	lazos
bracelet	pulsera
buttons	botones
coat	saco, chamarra
dress	vestido
gloves	guantes
handkerchief	pañuelo
hat	sombrero
hose, stockings	medias
jacket	chaqueta
necklace	collar
overcoat	abrigo
pants	pantalones
purse	bolsa
ring	anillo
scarf	bufanda
shirt	camisa
shoe	zapato
skirt	falda
sock	calcetín
suit	traje
sweater	suéter
tie	corbata
undershirt	camiseta
underwear	ropa interior

Cantos

(Tune: The Bear Went Over the Mountain)

Estos son mis zapatos,
Estos son mis zapatos,
Estos son mis zapatos,
tra, la, la, la, la, la, la.

These are my shoes,
These are my shoes,
These are my shoes,
tra, la, la, la, la, la, la.

Este es mi sombrero, etc.

This is my hat, etc.

Esta es mi faldita, etc.

This is my skirt, etc.

Esta es mi blusa, etc.

This is my blouse, etc.

Estos son mis pantalones, etc.

These are my pants, etc.

Esta es mi camisa, etc.

This is my shirt, etc.

Estos son mis calcetines, etc.

These are my socks, etc.

Sombreros
(hats)

Cut a large circle from craft paper for a brim. Cut an opening for the head and attach a crown to the brim and staple. Decorate with crayons.

Materials:
Two large sheets of butcher paper, string, scissors, wheat paste, crushed newspaper.

Directions:
1. Cover one sheet of butcher paper completely with wheat paste.

2. Place the second piece of butcher paper carefully over the first sheet and press.

3. Put the sheets while they are still damp on the head of a child shaping the crown of the sombrero.

4. Tie a string around the crown to hold it in place.

5. Stuff the crown with crushed newspaper and set the hat on the floor, smooth out the brim, trimming it where necessary to shape.

6. Turn the brim up as desired and let it dry thoroughly.

7. Carefully remove the string and newspapers and decorate.

Rebozo
(Shawl)

Materials:
 White or pastel crepe paper, crayons or markers, scissors.

Directions:

1. Cut out a 36" square from a sheet of crepe paper.

2. Using crayons or markers, color designs on the squares.

3. Fringe cut the edges.

4. Fold the rebozo in a triangle and wear it around you shoulders. Now you are ready to do the Jarabe Tapatio.

Note: This activity could be done with tie-dying, old material scraps etc.

 The rebozo is a shawl that is worn by the women around their shoulders. It is an important part of the China Poblana costume that is worn as the national dress. Women also use the rebozo to carry their babies.

From *COPYCAT MAGAZINE*, Copyright © 1988 Copycat Press, Inc. Racine, Wisconsin. Reprinted with Permission

Haraches
(Shoes)

Materials:

cardboard, reusable Handi-Wipes, scissors and a stapler.

Directions:

1. Draw around both the left and the right shoe.

2. Cut out the soles.

3. Cut four strips 4" x 7" of Handi-Wipe cloth.

4. Fold the strips in thirds making 1 1/2" x 7" strips.

5. Criss-cross the strips and staple the two pieces to each sole. Cut off the excess.

Haraches are leather sandles that are worn by the people in the small villages.

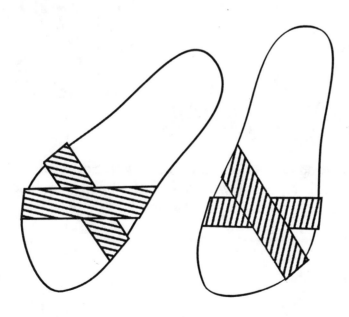

Bolero
(Jacket)

The bolero is the short jacket that is worn during fiestas. It is part of the charro costume that is worn by the "mariachi" or the men in the "Jarabe Tapatia" (Mexican Hat Dance).

Materials:
grocery bags, crayons, markers or paint, scissors and yarn.

Directions:
1. Cut armholes in the sides of the grocery bag, near the bottom of the bag.

2. Cut up the center of the front to neck.

3. Cut opening for neck. Test the size.

4. Cut to waist size and decorate with crayons or markers.

Serapes
(Woven Blankets)

Serapes can be made the same way but it can be longer. Paint colorful stripes on the bag. Slits can be made to weave yarn across the bag. Also, holes can be punched along the bottom and yarn can be attached for fringe.

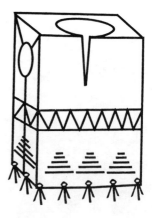

Games/Activities

Toro Toro

Players make a circle with one child in the center (toro). Children call to him/her, "Toro, Toro, are you ready?" Toro answers, "No, I must put on my (Spanish name for an article of clothing)!" Children call again and Toro says, "No, I must put on my (another piece of clothing)." Each time, Toro must do the motions of putting on the article of clothing he/she is saying. Suddenly, he says, "Here I come!" Children run to the safety area (a place that is chosen before the game) before Toro can tag them. When a child is tagged, he becomes Toro. Write the names of clothing on the board if played in the class or help the child with names if he/she needs help.

Mis Vecinos Me Encantan
(I Like My Neighbors)

The children sit in chairs in a circle. There is a chair for every student except one and that child stands in the middle. The child in the middle says, "Mis vecinos me encantan." (I love my neighbors.) Me encantan los que llevan _____. (I love my neighbors that wear _____ and they add an article of clothing in Spanish). For example: Me encantan mis vecinos a los que llevan zapatos de tenis. All the children that are wearing tennis shoes have to run around the inside of the chairs while the child joins them to find a chair. The child that is left without a chair has to stand in the middle and continues the game.

febrero

FEBRUARY

Fiestas
Comida

CELEBRATIONS
FOOD

febrero (February) Contents

February English/Spanish Vocabulary

apple	manzana	lemon	limón
bacon	tocino	liver	hígado
beans	frijoles	lobster	langosta
beef	carne de res	lunch	al muerzo
bread	pan	meat	carne
breakfast	desayuno	melon	melón
butter	mantequilla	milk	leche
cake	torta	onion	cebolla
carrots	zanahorias	orange	naranja
celery	apio	oysters	ostras
chicken	pollo	peas	guisantes
coffee	café	pepper	pimienta
cookies	galletas	pork	puerco
corn	maíz	potatoes	papas
crab	cangrejo	peach	melocotón
dessert	postre	radishes	rábanos
dinner	cena	rice	arroz
eggs	huevos	salad	ensalada
fig	higo	salt	sal
fish (out of water)	pescado	shrimp	camarones
food	comida	snack	la merienda
fork	tendor	spoon	cuchara
garlic	ajo	steak	bistec
grapes	uvas	strawberries	fresas
green beans	frijoles verdes	tea	té
ham	jamón	toast	pan tostado
ice cream	helado	tomato	tomate
jam	jalea	turkey	pavo
juice	jugo	vegetables	legumbres
knife	cuchillo	watermelon	sandía

Fiestas

Holidays and festivals are an integral part of any culture, but are a particularly important part of Mexican life. The blending of both Indian and Christian religious practices encourages celebrations as a way of keeping old traditions alive and fostering the growth of new ones. Mexico's history of political struggle, reform, and revolution is another catalyst for the remembrance of important days. "Fiestas" occur all over Mexico at many times during the year. There are many variations of the same celebration and customs may change from village to village. Most "fiestas" have in common a festive, fun ambience. There is almost always music, dancing, feasting, and decorations.

Religious Fiestas:

Día de los Reyes Magos: January 6, Day of the 3 Kings. Children receive small gifts. (See June for description.)

Día de San Antonio: January 17, Blessing of the Animals. (See June for description.)

Pascua: Easter (See June.)

Cuaresma: Lent, reenactment of the Passion Play during Semana Santa, Holy Week. (See June.)

Quinceñera: Special "Coming of Age" mass for 15 year old girls. (See June.)

Bodas: Wedding (See June.)

Día de Todos Los Santos: November 1, special mass for all the saints.

Día de Los Muertos: November 2, memorial mass for ancestors. Special celebration and preparation of graves. (See October.)

Día de la Virgen: December 12, celebration of the Virgen and her visit to the Indian, Juan Diego. (See November.)

Las Posadas: December 16 - December 24, reenactment of Mary and Joseph's search for lodging. (See December.)

Patriotic Fiestas:

Día de la Raza: October 12, Columbus Day. Celebration of the new race of Spanish and Indian heritage.

Día de Independencia: September 16, Celebration of "El Grito de Dolores," Father Hidalgo and Independence from Spain. (See September.)

Cinco de Mayo: May 5, Celebration of the victory of Mexican forces over the French invaders at Puebla. (See May.)

Candelaria

February 2, El Día de Candelaria or Candelmas Day signals the official end of the Christmas season. On this day the Church's yearly supply of candles is blessed, and a lullaby is sung to the baby Jesus before the Nacimiento is carefully put away for the year. In Mexico, Candelaria is a day for many Indian cultural festivities. The "Dance of the Deer" is traditional and a week long feast. Small images made from cornstalks are sold, celebrating the saint, Our Lady of Zapopan, who was said to have been made from the hearts of cornstalks. It is a time in which many Indians arrive in the cities in their native dress to participate in ceremonies and celebration.

Danza del Venado
(Dance of the Deer)

The deer, which is held sacred by the Yaqui and Mayan Tribes, is celebrated in this dance. The open plain is represented by a well-swept street. A pole represents the forest. The dance depicts the struggle between good and evil.

Two coyotes enter the scene, salute the musicians, and begin to dance. They wear masks covering one side of their faces. Around the waist, they wear a leather belt with bells, the trouser legs are covered with tiny rattles made of butterfly cocoons filled with pebbles.

The deer dancer stands in the center, ties a white handkerchief around his head, and shakes rattles he holds in his hands. As the music changes rhythm, the deer begins to dance and express his feelings of confusion. He sees danger as the coyotes draw near and the rhythm of his dance changes again. The sounds of the instruments and the dancers work together to suggest the sounds of the forest.

Fiesta Folkloria de Mexico-National Hispanic University

The History of Piñatas

The piñata is part of Mexican tradition and it is used at all celebrations or "fiestas."

Who would have ever thought that the piñata originally came from Italy over 400 years ago. During the 16th century, Italy was in the Renaissance. They were breaking away from the church and the rituals that had been such a part of their lives. It was more important to have fun.

The only people who could read or write were the rich people so everyone else had to amuse themselves. They invited lots of guests over and they played a lot of games. One of the games involved putting a blindfold on someone and then they would hang a clay pot in front of them and they would try to break the pot with a stick. The pot was called a "pignatta" which meant cone-shapped.

In Spain, however, things were more serious and the people were more concerned with the church. They set-aside the first Sunday of Lent as "Piñata" Sunday. This was called the "Pascua de Cuaresma." "Cuaresma" or Lent was and still is a time of fasting and penances. The people held a masquerade ball where they danced the "flamenco," the "bolero," or the "zarabanda." The Ball was called the Dance of the "Piñata." During the dance, the piñata was broken.

The Spanish version of the piñata referred to the game rather than the pot for their pot is called an "olla." The pot was so ugly and plain that the people began to put something around the pot to make it look more attractive. There is no exact date when the piñata came to Mexico; however, it is felt that it came over with the early settlers in New Spain. The main difference in customs is that it is an Easter tradition in Spain, and in Mexico, it is more popular at Christmas.

The piñata did not change much until about fifty years ago when the people began making different piñatas in different shapes and out of different materials.

Another change came with the tourism in Mexico. Tourists wanted more piñatas than they could personally make and so it became a business.

Since the piñata came to Mexico, it has been filled with candies and sweets for the children. It may also include nuts, fruits and other types of treats.

There is a legend that states that the piñata symbolizes evil and the children are good. When a child breaks the piñata, then goodness overcomes evil and the world receives the many blessings (the treats).

One guest, chosen by the host/hostess, is blindfolded and led to the spot beneath the piñata. Traditionally, he/she was handed a broomstick (with everyone else standing at a distance) and he/she takes a big swing. Some people raise and lower the piñata or give it a big swing to make it more difficult. Also, the person doing the hitting can be turned around before trying to hit the piñata. Usually, he/she gets three swings and if he/she does not break the piñata, the blindfold and the stick go to the next person.

In Tuscany, the game is a little different in that they hang three piñatas close together and one is filled with water, one with ashes and one with treats.

Another variation in Italy is called "pentolaccia" where all the treats go to the person who broke the piñata.

Nowadays, the piñata is played all over the world at different times or reasons. The main thing is that it is a custom that is colorful and fun and one that young and old alike enjoy.

Be creative and celebrate your Mexico unit with a piñata. It does not have to be a holiday and the piñata does not have to hold candies. Here are some suggestions:

1. New Years: Make a piñata full of noise makers and hats.

2. Valentines Day: Make a heart filled with cards.

3. St. Patrick's Day: Make a shamrock filled with gold chocolate coins and "green" treats.

4. Easter: Make an Easter egg filled with confetti.

5. Birthday party: Make a cake filled with little presents.

6. Graduation: Make a star and fill it with diplomas and pennies.

La Piñata

An - da - le   Pe - pe   no   pier - das   el
ti - no _____ que   de   la   dis   tan - cia   se
pier - de   el   cami - no   con   los   o - ji - tos   ven-
da - dos y   en   las   ma - nos   un   bas - ton ___
Se ha - ce   la   olli - ta   peda - zos   sin - ten - er   le   com - pasión   da - le   da - le   dal - le   no   pier - das   el
ti - no   que   de   la   dis -   tan - cia   se   pierde   el   ca - mi - no.

Andale, Pepe, no pierdas el tino
Que de la distancia se pierde el camino.
Con los ojitos vendidos y en las
    manos un bastón.
Se hace la ollita pedazos sin tenerle
    compasión.
Dale, dale, dale, no pierdas
    el tino,
Que de la distancia se pierde
    el camino.

Come on, Pepe, don't lose
    your touch,
Which from the distance misses
    the direction.
With your eyes blindfolded
    and a stick in your hand.
Break the jar to pieces
    without compassion.
Hit it, hit it, hit it, don't
    lose your touch,
Which from a distance misses
    the direction.

Piñata

Quick and Easy

1. Decorate a brown grocery bag with strips of fringed crepe paper (4" wide). Glue them by overlapping the strips and curling the ends around a pencil.

3. Fill the bag with "goodies' and tie the end.

4. Or, add a top to the piñata such as a birds head and wings and add a tail for color.

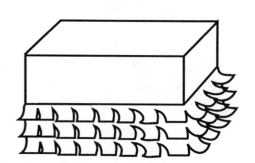

Luncheon Sacks

1. Cut a luncheon sack in half across the middle.

2. Take a sheet of white or colored paper and fold it in half.

3. Trace the pattern of a parrot or other design, and cut it out. Do the same thing with the head pattern.

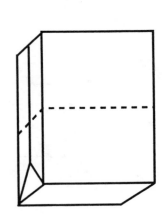

4. Paste one side of the body to each side of the bag.

5. Paste one head part to each side.

6. Cut crepe paper into thin strips or streamers and use them for the tail and wings.

From *MEXICAN*, by Barbara Schubert and Marlene Bird. Copyright © 1976. A Reflections & Images Publication. San Jose, California. Reprinted with permission.

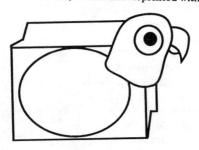

Piñatas-Balloons

It is possible to make piñatas by using balloons that are blown up. Tear newspapers into strips and dip into wheat paste or liquid laundry starch. Cover the balloons to the desired shape. Tearing the paper is more effective because the rough edges help the paper stick together. Reinforce the area between two balloons if they are used by placing the strips lengthwise between the two balloons. Four layers of strips are enough. Leave an opening to be closed after the piñata has dried so you can put the treat in. Then seal the piñata and decorate with crepe paper strips that are curled at the ends.

Arms and legs can be added but need to be done so while the piñata is wet. Make an animal, person, bird etc.

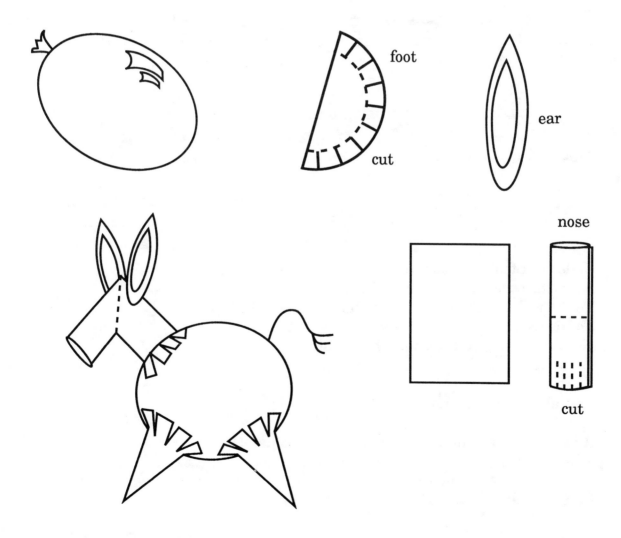

foot

cut

ear

nose

cut

La Raspa

(a version)

Res - ba-le a-sí su pie   un-os dos y tres

A la de - re - cha   a-la-de - re - cha,
A la iz - quier-da   a la iz - quier-da

a la de - re - cha   a-la-de - re - cha
a la iz - quier-da,   a la iz - quier - da

Buen - os   di - as   niño

bue - nos   dia - s   ni - ño   ra - mos a bai-

lar_____   y tam - bien a can - tar.

Slide your foot, one, two, three,
Now, the other foot, one, two, three,
To the right, to the right, to the right, to the right,
To the left, to the left, to the left, to the left.
Good morning child, good morning child,
We are going to dance and also to sing.

Resbale así su pie, uno, dos, tres,
Ahora el otro pie, uno, dos, tres.
A la derecha, a la derecha, a la derecha, a la derecha.
A la izquierda, a la izquierda, a la izquierda, a la izquierda.
Buenos días niño, buenos niño,
Vamos a bailar y también a cantar.

Tacos

The word "taco" means snack in Spanish but today is used to denote the sandwich type dish below. Tortillas, which have been folded and fried are filled with meat or beans, a spicy sauce, and cheese, lettuce or tomatoes.

Ingredients:

1 dozen corn tortillas
vegetable oil for frying
2 cups ground, cooked meat
shredded lettuce, chopped tomatoes, grated cheddar or jack cheese
bottled salsa or "salsa cruda" (see recipe)

Directions:

1. Heat oil and fry tortilla lightly on one side. Turn over with tongs, and fold in half. Fry both sides until lightly crisp.

2. Drain on paper towels, continue with remaining tortillas.

3. Fill taco shells with meat and desired condiments.

4. Beans, peppers, and onion are excellent additions as well.

Serves 4

Salsa Cruda
(Chunky Salsa)

Ingredients:
- 2 lbs. ripe tomatoes
- 1 large onion
- 1 can green chilies
- 1 tsp. chopped cilantro (fresh coriander), if available
- 1 can tomatillos (optional – found in import section)
- 1 clove minced garlic
- 1 tsp. oregano
- 1/4 tsp. cumin
- 2 Tbsp. olive oil
- 2 Tbsp. wine vinegar
- salt and pepper to taste

Directions:

Peel and chop tomatoes and onion; rinse seeds from chiles, and chop. Add cilantro. Mash tomatillos and combine with other tomatoes, onions and chiles. Add the rest of the ingredients. Chill to blend flavors. Serve with meats and Mexican dishes.

Quesadillas
(Cheese Tortillas)

These cheese tortillas make great snacks!

Sprinkle grated monterey jack cheese on half of a flour tortilla. Fold over, toast in 350° oven 10 minutes or microwave on high for 45 seconds and enjoy!

Tortillas De Maíz

Mix 2 cups "masa harina" (finely ground cornmeal found in the import section of your market or with the flour products) with 1 1/2 cups warm water, then form into balls about 1 3/4 inches in diameter. Roll between sheets of plastic or oiled waxed paper into thin, round pancakes 6 inches in diameter. Cook on lightly greased, medium hot griddle, turning frequently until dry and lightly flecked with brown.

Tortillas De Harina

Sift together 4 cups flour and 2 tsp. salt. Work in 1/3 cup lard (or shortening) with fingertips, then stir in enough water to form into a ball. Knead until smooth and form into egg sized balls. Cover and let stand 20 minutes. Roll out to 7 or 8 inches. Cook as for the corn tortillas on a medium hot griddle. These are delicious warm with butter, fried, or as they are used in a variety of Mexican dishes.

Menudo

Mexicans adore Menudo, which means "minced" or "cut into small pieces." This soup is traditionally served on Christmas or New Year's Eve although it is eaten throughout the year.

Ingredients:

    5 lbs. tripe
    1 large veal knuckle
    4 garlic cloves, cut
    3 tsp. salt
    2 cups chopped onions
    1 tsp ground coriander
    1 Tbsp. chili powder
    1 can peeled green chilis, chopped
    2 qts. water
    2 1/2 cups (1 lb. 13 oz. can) hominy
    Juice of 1 lemon

Cooking Directions:

Cut tripe into 3/4 inch strips. Mix all ingredients, except hominy and lemon juice, in a large pot and simmer for 6 hours, until tripe is tender. Add more water if needed. Add hominy to heat through. Add lemon juice and serve with chopped green onions and cilantro.

Serves 6-8

Enchiladas Con Pollo

Enchiladas are rolled tortillas which may be filled with any combination of meat, cheese, and/or vegetables, and topped with sauce and cheese. We have included our version below, but do not be afraid to experiment with your own ideas!

Basic Recipe:
8 corn tortillas
2 Tbsp. oil
sauce, warmed
filling
cheese

Cooking Directions:
1. Heat oil in skillet and fry tortilla for a few seconds.

2. Remove tortilla and dip in sauce.

3. Set in baking dish and fill with about 1/4 cup filling. Roll and place with opening faced down.

4. When all the tortillas are filled, cover with remaining sauce. Bake at 350° until bubbly (about 20 minutes). Top with additional cheese the last 10 minutes.

5. Serve with sour cream, if desired.

Chicken and Cheese Filling:
2 large chicken breasts
2 Tbsp. vegetable oil
1 large onion, chopped
1 large green pepper, chopped
1/2 tsp oregano
1/2 tsp. basil
2 1/2 cups grated monterey jack, or cheddar cheese.

Cooking Instructions:
1. Simmer chicken in 3 cups water 20 minutes, until done.

2. Saute onion and green pepper with oregano and basil until vegetables are soft.

3. Drain chicken, remove bones, and slice meat.

4. Place strip of chicken in middle of tortilla, spoon on 2 Tbsp. of vegetable mixture, and roll up.

5. Pour on additional sauce.

Enchilada Sauce

You may use canned sauce, in which case you will need 3 cups, or below is an easily prepared recipe using chili powder.

Ingredients:
  1 medium onion, chopped
  2 Tbsp. oil
  3 1/2 cups tomato puree
  2 cloves garlic
  4 Tbsp. chili powder
  1/2 tsp. ground cumin
  1/4 tsp. oregano
  1 tsp. salt

Cooking Directions:
  1. Saute onion until soft, add tomato puree and garlic.

  2. Gradually stir in chili powder, cumin, oregano, and salt.

  3. Cover and simmer about 30 minutes, stirring occasionally.

  Makes 3 cups.

Sopa Seca
(Mexican Rice)

Arroz Mexicano, Mexican rice, often referred to as "sopa" belongs to a group of dishes called dry soups. A dry soup is made by cooking a starchy food, such as rice or tortillas, slowly in broth until the liquid is completely absorbed. Serve the "sopa" as part of a Mexican meal before the meat course.

Ingredients:
    1 cup white rice, uncooked
    2 Tbsp. oil
    4 cups tomato juice
    4 Tbsp. butter
    1/2 tsp. ground cumin
    1 tsp. salt
    1/2 green pepper, chopped
    2 garlic cloves, minced
    1 1/2 cups chopped onion
    2 large tomatoes, chopped (or 1 cup canned)

Cooking Directions:
1. Rinse and drain rice. Dry on paper towels.

2. Heat oil in frying pan and saute rice until golden.

3. Heat tomato juice in saucepan and add the rice.

4. Add the rest of the ingredients, cover, and simmer over low heat until juice is absorbed and rice is soft (20-30 minutes).

Serves 4-6

Tamales

Tamales are made of cornmeal dough which is spread on cornhusks, then filled, and steamed.

When corn is in season tamales may be made with the fresh corn husks instead of the usual dried ones. Tamales may be sweet or spicy, but always a delicious treat.

Ingredients:
1 3/4 cups "masa," fine corn flour
1 cup warm water
1/2 tsp. salt
1/4 cup lard or shortening
fresh or dried corn husks
1 cup fresh or canned corn
1/2 cup cheddar cheese
2 canned green chili peppers, chopped
1/2 tsp. salt

Cooking Directions:
1. Mix the first 4 ingredients together to form a smooth paste.

2. Wash corn husks. Set aside 2 husks for each tamale.

3. Paste the 2 husks together with a bit of the masa. Spread the inside of the husks with a layer of masa, leaving a 1 inch border at the top and bottom.

4. Combine the last 4 ingredients to make the corn-cheese filling.

5. Put 2 tsp. filling in each of the tamales, fold husk around the filling and seal with a little more masa.

6. Stand tamales in a steamer and steam for an hour.

   Makes 1 dozen.

Frijoles
(Mexican Beans)

Beans are as important to the Mexican diet as tortillas.

Ingredients:
  1 lb. Mexican pink or pinto beans
  6 cups water
  1/2 tsp. ground cumin
  2 garlic cloves
  2 tsp. salt
  2 Tbsp. bacon fat or lard

Cooking Directions:

Cover beans with water, add cumin, garlic, and simmer over low heat for 1 1/2 hours. Add salt, fat, and continue to simmer until beans are tender.

Serves 6

Arroz Con Leche

Rice pudding is a favorite Mexican dessert. We have also included a traditional children's rhyme:

Arroz con Leche

Arroz con leche, me quiero casar
    con una viudita de la capital.
Que sepa coser, que sepa bordar,
    que ponga la mesa en su santo lugar.
Yo soy la viudita, la hija de Rey,
    me quiero casar y no hallo con quien.
Contigo sí, contigo no
    contigo, mi vida, me casaré yo!

Ingredients:
1/2 cup white rice, uncooked
1/2 cinnamon stick
1 1/2 cups water
1 cup sweetened condensed milk
2 1/2 Tbsp. raisins
cinnamon

Cooking Directions:
1. Put rice, cinnamon stick, and water in a saucepan. Bring to a boil, reduce heat, cover and simmer until water is absorbed (about 15 minutes).

2. Add milk and raisins. Cook uncovered, until milk is absorbed into rice (about 15 minutes).

3. Remove from the heat, take out cinnamon stick, and cover. Let sit for about 10 minutes. Sprinkle with cinnamon.

marzo
MARCH

arte
deportes
ART
SPORTS

marzo (March) Contents

March English/Spanish Vocabulary

art	arte
balance	equilibrio
brush	pincel
brush stroke	pincelado
color	color
to color	colorar
contour	contorno
to copy	copiar
crayon	crayón
to create	crear
to develop (themselves)	desarrollarse
development	desarrollo
to draw	dibujar
environment	medio ambiente
light	luz
line	línea
mix	mezclar
mixture	mezcla
oil paint	óleo
(done in) oil paint	al óleo
to outline	delinear
paint	pintura
to paint	pintar
pencil	lápiz
picture, portrait	retrato
rhythm	ritmo
shadow	sombra
synthetic/acrylic paint	pintura sintética/acrílica
tempera paint	témpera
texture	textura
tone	tono
to trace	trazar
watercolor	acuarela
work of art	obra
work of art/picture	cuadro

Arte
(Art)

Mexico has a wonderful and varied artistic tradition. It is neither wholly Indian nor European, but rather a blending of the most beautiful techniques from the two cultures. It would be impossible, in a book such as this, to introduce adequately every area of Mexican art. This is just a sampling of our favorites. We hope you will find the information helpful and the activities enriching.

The Indians in Mexico comprise over half of the population. They have incorporated a sense of beauty into the crafts which they have refined. Often isolated in villages far away from roads and cities, the Indian looks to nature for his inspiration and uses his hands to create art he can both admire and use in his daily life.

Before the Spanish conquest in 1521, many Indian peoples including the Mayas and the Aztecs produced splendid objects of art. Much of this was destroyed during the conquest and it is only through the work of archeologists that we are able to gain a sense of the great treasures which existed during this time.

After the conquest, the Indians were needed for agricultural tasks and construction. They were not permitted to adorn churches or other buildings with paintings. The Indians were permitted to create needed items such as pottery, textiles, lacquer and leather articles, and in this way found a place to continue the creative process.

The true splendor of Indian art was not appreciated by the Mexican upper classes until after the Revolution of 1910. The nationalism of this period encouraged Mexicans to look within their own country for inspiration and beauty. The government encouraged the work of gifted artists. The influence of Indian culture on music and dance also gained recognition at this time and became an integral part of Mexican festivals and tradition.

Huichol Yarn Painting

Wool was unknown in Mexico before the Conquest. Fibers from native plants such as cotton, cactus, and maguey were spun into thread with a "malacate" or clay whorl. As wool became the primary source of thread for Mexican looms, skillful Indian weavers created incredible patterns using native dyes. The native loom, "telar de otate," is horizontal with one end tied to a post and the other end attached to a belt around the weaver's waist.

The Huichol Indians, from the state of Jalisco, create marvelous textiles in wool. Their inaccessibility in the mountains of the Sierra Madre, have enabled them to maintain many of the traditional techniques and motifs which make their work so distinctive. They place colored yarn on beeswax to create designs which are called "faces of the world." They may refer to legends of the gods or their hopes for a fruitful crop or hunt. These plaques are placed on home altars as offerings to the gods. Animal motifs are often part of the design.

This artistic work is part of the religious ritual of the Huichol. To please the fire god and to receive inspiration from the hallucinatory properties of the cactus, the Indians often chew "peyote" while creating their "paintings."

Yarn Paintings

Materials:
Bulky knitting wool in black, scraps of knitting wool in other bright colors, thick cardboard, tracing paper, pencil, tape, white glue and scissors.

Directions:
1. Trace a pattern and transfer it onto the cardboard holding the tracing paper in place with tape.

2. Squeeze a thin line of glue on short part of the outline. Cut a piece of black wool and glue it. Continue with the black until the outline is complete.

3. Fill in small sections inside the outline and glue the yarn in ever-decreasing circles.

4. Fill in the background the last of all.

Crewel Embroidery can be done as an activity. Sometimes, it is easier to staple the material onto a wooden frame before stitching. Cross-stitching is possible using yarns.

Fake Yarn Paintings

A technique that gives the effect of the yarn paintings is also possible especially with the younger children.

Materials:
paper, black crayon and other colors.

Directions:
1. Draw the design and outline it in black bold lines. Color between the black lines carefully. If the motor coordination is needed, then, start with the coloring and then add the black outlines.

Tissue and Yarn

Materials:
yarn, scissors, starch, wax paper, newsprint, colored tissue paper, white glue.

Directions:
1. Sketch a design or figure on a 9" x 12" newsprint.

2. Go over the outline with a black crayon.

3. Cover drawing with wax paper, dip yarn in a glue-starch mixture and place it over the crayon lines.

4. Two or three pieces of yarn together side by side add strength. Lift off the wax paper and glue the tissue to the yarn.

Yarn Art Pots

Materials:
small can (juice cans are good), heavy twine or yarn of different colors, white glue, scissors.

Directions:
1. Use the can as your base.

2. Put one inch of glue around the base of the can.

3. Wrap the yarn around the can evenly. Begin at the bottom and work your way up.

4. Another inch of glue is added and the procedure continues.

Note: The yarns should vary in color for variety and they do not have to be straight. A curved line is sometimes most artistic. Also, plastic bottles may be used with the tops cut off or not – depends on the use. The plastic bottle can be used as a vase.

Scribble Yarn Art

Materials:
colored magazine ads, white construction paper, black yarn, glue, watercolor or crayons.

Directions:

1. With a yellow crayon, make a scribble on the paper.

2. Tear colored magazine ads into small pieces and glue them into one of the shapes. Use a different colored ad in each shape.

3. Outline each shape with a thin line of glue and fasten down black yarn.

4. Color the area around the design with crayons or watercolors.

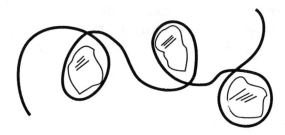

Wool Wrappings

Make a necklace or belt by braiding several strands of wool yarn together. Leave some fringe at each end.

Make a bundle of yarn and tie it at the end by wrapping it with wool, following the diagrams.

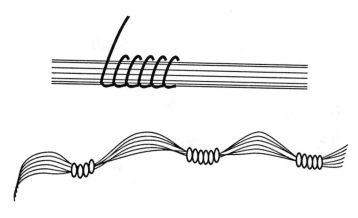

Ojo de Dios
(Eye of God)

The Ojo de Dios is the most recognizable art form in Mexico. It is meant to protect the children so it is a perfect project for any classroom.

Materials:
two sticks about 6" long, different colored yarns (3 ply).

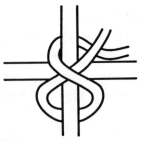

Directions:
1. Tie the sticks together to form a cross. See diagrams.

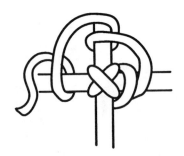

2. Bringing the yarn from underneath, wind it around the top of the right-hand stick, under it, then over to the next up-right stick. Wind yarn over, then round again to the next stick.

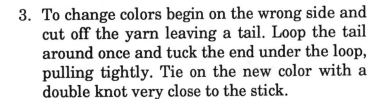

3. To change colors begin on the wrong side and cut off the yarn leaving a tail. Loop the tail around once and tuck the end under the loop, pulling tightly. Tie on the new color with a double knot very close to the stick.

4. Continue with the new color as before.

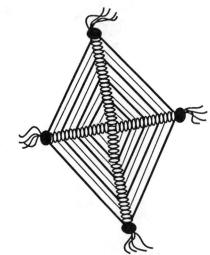

5. To finish the star, knot the yarn around the stick and cut off neatly.

6. At the end of the sticks, tie a piece of yarn for extra decoration.

Pottery

Fortunately, because of its durable character, there are many examples of pre-conquest pottery still in existence in Mexico today. The ancient potters utilized almost all of the same techniques used by modern potters. Some of the most beautiful pottery in Mexico was created by Toltec, Maya, Zapotec, Mixtec, and Aztec artists. The form, color, and style of their work rivals modern creations.

The Spanish brought their own techniques including; the wheel, glazing, and kiln firing, which the Indian artists incorporated into their work.

There are many kinds of pottery in Mexico but it is usually defined as either "corriente," common, or "caro," expensive for city people. Whole villages may engage in the industry of making common pottery. It is usually glazed and comes in all of the forms important in meeting the needs of the poor. There are "cazuelas," large bowls for meats, water jars, dishes and every manner of bowl or utensil needed for everyday living.

Expensive pottery is usually sold in the cities, and often emphasizes decoration over a practical use.

Pottery From Tonalá

There is a valley in the state of Jalisco, near Guadalajara in which two of the finest centers of Mexican pottery making are located. The earth in the valley of Atemajac is such that Tonalá and Tlaquepaue have been creating fine pottery since ancient times.

One can find an incredible variety of objects, including figures for a Nacimiento or Nativity scene. The common characteristics are; the color of the fine red clay, the soft grey which results from a complicated process called "varnishing," and the indigenous motifs depicting nature. The pottery may be made by hand or on a potter's wheel.

Clay Toys From Metepec

Metepec, in the state of Mexico is famous for its clay which is said to be as fine as that found in the Valley of Atemajac. This pottery center is famous for its small toy figures which were originally used as part of religious rituals. Today artists in Metepec produce toys in modern, as well as the traditional, motifs for use as decoration in the homes of Mexican families.

Coyotepec Pottery

The state of Oaxaca is one of the richest regions for native handicrafts in Mexico. The geographical variety and the many indigenous communities who inhabit this state have been the perfect combination for a region rich in cultural diversity.

One of the most interesting crafts created in Oaxaca is the pottery of Coyotepec. The distinctive black polished surfaces and the use of human and animal figures to make all kinds of bowls, pictures, strainers or "pichanchas," and even whistles are unique.

Tonalá Pottery Project

The one thing that makes the Tonalá pottery so unique is the style of the painting. Every piece is hand-painted and is done with exquisite detail.

Materials:
clay or self-hardening clay, paints.

Directions:
Make figures or models of owls, birds, nacimiento (nativity) figures and paint them according to the Tonalá designs. Characteristic of their art could be a whole landscape and the dress of a figure. See below for ideas.

rust - dark blue
designs

gray - blue
backgrounds

earth tones

Tree of Life
(Symbol of the Pueblo Indians)

Materials:
Self-hardening modeling clay or Mexican pottery clay, wooden rod, 10-12" long, iron wire (coat hangers), large pebble, matt white water-base paint, gouache, varnish.

Directions:
1. Cut pieces of iron wire and wrap them around the wooden rod, spacing them as in the drawing. Attach each piece securely.

2. Stand the assembly up on a large pebble embedded in a thick layer of modeling clay. Make a base large enough to keep the tree standing securely.

3. Work the clay into several sausage shaped rolls. Use these to cover the wire.

4. Cover the central trunk with small pieces of clay.

5. Spread this layer evenly over the entire surface of the tree. (Use a wooden spatula, tongue depressor or other modeling tool.) Be careful of hollow spots or areas that are too thick. Also, be careful to smooth around branch joints.

6. With your fingers, shape the objects to go on the tree.

7. Moisten the spot where they are to go and the spot on the object so that they will adhere together.

8. Let it dry for several days before painting.

9. If cracks develop, fill them in with fresh clay and continue to let them dry.

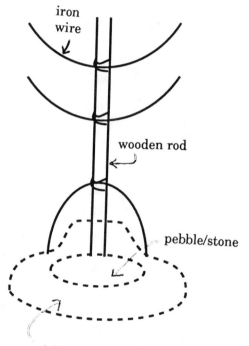

iron wire

wooden rod

pebble/stone

modeling compound

Tree of life (cont.)

Decoration:

1. Paint a coat of matt white paint and let it dry. Be sure to cover the entire tree.

2. Decorate with gouache paints in bright, bold colors.

3. After it is dry, you can cover it with varnish to protect it.

Tree of Life

Materials:
Two 6" or 9" plates, ruler, pencil, scissors, one 8 1/2" x 11" sheet of white drawing paper, paste or glue, felt-tipped pens, pattern ornaments (if desired).

Directions:
1. Using ruler and pencil, draw lines dividing one paper plate into 8 equal parts. (Lines should not be more than 2" long.)
2. Cut along lines A-B, C-D etc. This will be the base of your tree.

3. Cut out the center to form a ring. (2nd plate.)

4. Roll drawing paper into a tube approximately 1" in diameter and secure with paste or glue.

5. Decorate base, ring and tube with felt-tipped pens.

6. Draw tube through opening in center of base and secure with paste or glue. Paste ring onto tube.

7. Paste figures onto tube.

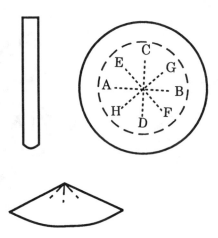

Basketry

Basket weaving is an art form which began even before pottery in Mexico. It is still an important occupation among many Indian and Mestizo groups.

Lake regions, where the availability of reeds and leaves are plentiful, are the primary centers of this craft. Patzcuaro is one such area which specializes in reed sleeping mats, petate, which are used by the general population. The tule reed is used to make this product, as well as many others such as toys, baskets, and fans. Palm reeds are used to create sombreros and baskets of exquisite design from the valley of Toluca. The fiber of the maguey plant is used to make hammocks and mats used under riding saddles.

Hot Dish Holder

Materials:
33 ice cream sticks, elastic thread, small drill, large eyed needle, 33 colored beads.

Directions:
Drill two holes in each stick as shown. Using the needle and thread, go through each hole near the end of the stick and tie securely. Do the same with the center holes, only alternate with the needle through a bean and then a stick. Tie securely. Wood may be painted or varnished before threading.

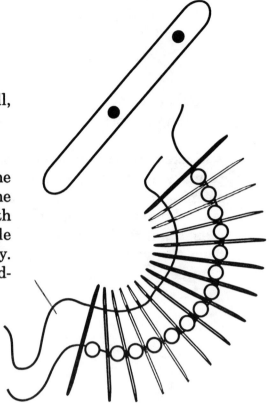

Berry Baskets

The Mexican artist have woven elaborate baskets from straw or grasses to decorate their homes, to carry food and to store things.

Tape one end of a bulky yarn as a needle and weave it through the openings on berry baskets. Simple yet decorative. Be sure to use different colors and bright ones, too.

Place Mats

Using two or more colors of construction paper, weave a placemat. Cut uniform slits in one piece and have many color strips of paper to use to weave. Laminate the finished project and use them as gifts or for placemats.

Cut slits

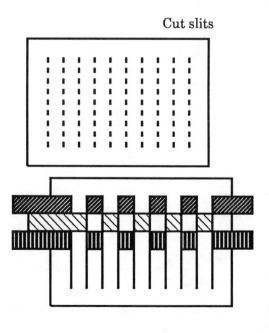

Metalwork

Silver craft is believed to have been introduced to Mexico by Central and South American silversmiths during the 10th century. Silver objects were in great demand during the colonial period and reached a degree of excellence unequaled since. During the second half of the 19th century, the interest in silver work declined. It was not until 1931, when a young American artist, William Spratling opened a silver workshop in Taxco, that the revival of Mexican silvercraft began. Taxco flourishes today, and the creation of magnificent silver pieces is once again a part of the Mexican artists' realm.

Tin work began in the colonial era when the Spanish hunger for precious metals caused shortages of silver and gold. Mexican artists began using tin, because of its availability and flexibility. The tin crafters or "hojaleteros" make a wide variety of objects whose beauty adorns the homes of Mexicans.

Iron was introduced by the Spaniards. The finest examples of ironwork were produced during the colonial period. Today there is handwrought iron everywhere in Mexico. Some of the best work is done creating machetes, long wide straight or curved knives. They are often adorned with decorations or an inscription such as, "If this reptile bites you, there is no cure in the drugstore."

Silver Necklace

Paint macaroni silver. Dry thoroughly and string.

Silver Charms

Materials:
4" square cardboard, aluminum foil (larger than the cardboard, heavy yarn scraps or cord, scissors, pattern, pencil.

Directions:
1. Trace the pattern on the cardboard. Cut it out and glue the yarn pieces on the cardboard. Place the yarn on the details and lines you want raised or outlined.

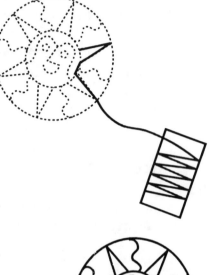

2. Place the foil over the yarn and gently mold it around the yarn so that the features are raised.

3. Tuck the edges behind the cardboard in back and glue them down.

4. Punch a hole at the top and put a string through the hole to wear it as a charm.

Note:
Black tempera paint can be brushed over the design to give it a burnished look.

Lacquerware

Lacquerware is usually lacquered first, dried and then the design is carved into the laquer. It is then rubbed with different colors. The following method is more suitable to the classroom.

Materials:
6" or 9" paper plate, crayons, black tempera, brush and water

Directions:
1. Draw and color a design in the center of the plate with brightly colored crayons. Press very hard so that the wax is thick and the colors are very bright.

2. With black tempera paint, brush over and paint the entire plate, including the design.

3. Let it dry thoroughly.

4. If a shine is desired, paint it with a mixture of white glue and water and let it dry.

Mask Hanging

Materials:
cardboard rectangle 8" x 5 1/2", piece of burlap (the same size), sheet of heavy metal foil for embossing (copper or aluminum), pencil, glue.

Directions:
1. Using tracing paper to transfer half of the mask to the metal foil, simply turning the paper over to transfer the right side of the pattern. (Use the pencil or a felt tip pen.)

2. With the point of a ball point pen trace the important parts of the silhouette, pressing down lightly (do not push through the metal sheet). Make the strongest lines with the handle of a paintbrush.

3. As you work, remember that each indented line you make appears as a raised line on the other side, which is the side you will display. It is a good idea to check the other side as you work to check your results.

4. Use embroidery scissors to cut out the eyes and mouth and open parts.

5. Glue the burlap flat on the front of the board. Glue on the mask.

6. You may want to put a thin layer of cotton fabric between the metal and cardboard to heighten the effect.

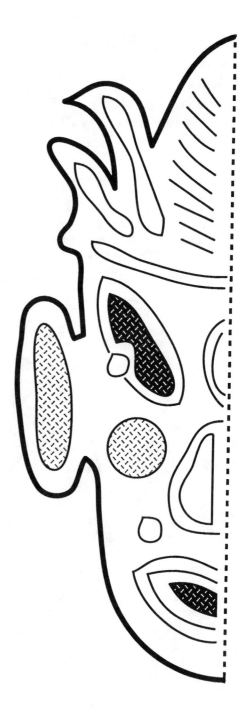

Lacquer

Lacquer is an art which was practiced in Mexico prior to the Spanish conquest. Some researchers believe it was introduced by the Chinese who are thought to have visited Mexico a thousand years before Cortés. The centers of lacquerware are located where the Chinese landed, in Michoacán and Guerrero. Whatever the origin, Mexican lacquerware exhibits its own character.

Lacquerware has developed in Michoacán and Guerrero partially because of two important elements. First the availability of the Chia seed and of the worm, gie, from which the Indians extract an oil which gives the lacquer a hard, waterproof surface. Second, the region has a plentiful supply of wood used for making the traditional large trays or "bateas."

The process begins by lacquering a black background on the wood and allowing it to dry. A design is then cut into the lacquer with a very fine point. Colors are applied one by one, with the palm of the hand. The arrival of the Spaniards did not change the process, but did add to the array of colors used by lacquer artists.

Lacquerware from Olinalá in the state of Guerrero is famous for its chests and "jícaras" gourds. The large chests used to be made from the aloe tree, whose wood carries a pleasant scent. Today, due to the scarcity of the tree, other woods are used and the chests are artificially scented. The "jícaras" are charming and inexpensive works of art, decorated inside and out with flowers or birds.

Bark Painting

Materials:
brown grocery bag (or butcher block paper), brightly colored tempera paints, brown tempera paint, paint brushes (some should be fine points), water and pencil.

Directions:
1. Tear off the edges of the paper to give a rough finish.

2. Crush the rectangle several times and then smooth it out.

3. Draw a design lightly with the pencil.

4. Paint the design in and let it dry.

5. After the paint is dry, take a dry brush and brush the background to give it a leather rough looking finish.

6. Let it dry thoroughly and then hang it.

Masks

The mask is a traditional medium found everywhere in Mexico. It may be used for secular or religious purposes and may be created from a myriad of materials. A mask is able to transform reality for both the wearer and the observer into the imaginative world of myths, legends and gods.

When the Spaniards arrived in Mexico, masks were used by the indigenous people as an integral part of the religious ritual and ceremony. These masks often carried magical properties to invoke the favor of the gods. Fortunately many of these early stone masks have survived and are displayed in Mexican museums. Many of the ancient forms were soon replaced by the Christian influence of the Spaniards. The Ancient ceremonies survived only in areas remote from the priests and the army.

Most Mexican masks focus on the human face. This concentration has developed masks which reveal the gamut of human emotions and expressions. In remote areas, masks of animals and devils are also important forms.

Archeologists have unearthed masks of metal, clay and stone. We know from Spanish writers that artists used other materials such as wood and leather, as well. Today masks may be make from wood, paper mache, metal, ceramics or any material the artist finds imaginative.

Masks

Nose Mask

Materials:
ball of string or raffia, egg cup, aluminum foil, white glue, mixing cup for glue, tablespoon, elastic thread, old newspaper

Directions:
1. Cover the egg cup with foil. Pin and coil string or raffia around it.

2. Mix a spoonful of white glue with two spoonfuls of water. Brush on and leave overnight. Paint on more glue mixture.

3. When it is dry you will see that the coiled string keeps its shape when you pull it off.

4. Thread the elastic through the edge of the nose shape, take it around your head and tie it to the other side. Do not make it too tight or it will pull the nose apart.

Paper Bag Masks

Materials:
paper bag or plate, scissors, crayons, yarn, string, straws, or anything from the junk drawer

Directions:
1. Measure the bag or plate for the position of the eyes and mark it with a pencil.

2. Draw or color a face on the bag or plate.

3. Cut eye holes.

4. Use yarn, straws or string for hair.

5. For the plate, punch holes on the sides and tie a piece of string in each hole.

Papier Mache Masks

Materials:

balloon (depends on the size of the students), newspaper strips, wheat paste, tempera paints, paint brushes, small, sharp kitchen knife, scissors, clear lacquer, two 18" lengths of string

Directions:

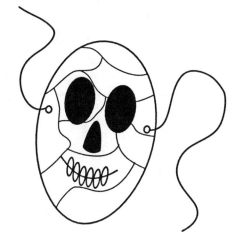

1. Mix the wheat paste according to package directions.

2. Cover balloon with five to seven layers of wheat paste. Dip each strip in the wheat before adding to the balloon. Wipe off excess paste.

3. Allow three to four days for drying. Stick a pin in the sculpture to burst the balloon.

4. With the knife, cut the papier mache mask in half. (Teacher-assisted.)

5. Cut eye holes and string holes.

6. Paint with the tempera paints the desired designs.

7. Spray with lacquer (clear).

8. Tie the string through the holes os that it is possible to matt these on a board for a wall hanging.

Note:

These can be made with modeling clay as a base for the papier mache as well as the balloon. Be sure the features are exaggerated as the paper strips will level out the forms.

Recipe:

One cup salt, 1/2 cup flour and one cup water. Heat over a low flame and stir until the mixture is thick and rubbery. If it is too sticky, add more flour. After it cools, it can be molded just like regular clay.

Deportes (Sports)

The ancient peoples of Mexico liked games. Three games which are known to have been enjoyed by the Maya and Aztecs are: Tlachtli, Patolli, and The Flying Pole game. Tlachtli is a ball game played on an enclosed court built in the form of an H. It is played by two teams of varying numbers. The ball may be hit with the elbow, hip or thigh, but may not touch the hands or feet. Each side of the court contains a large stone ring attached to the side wall. The team able to get the hard rubber ball through the ring first, wins the game. The Maya described the game in their sacred book, Popul Vuh, in terms of 2 heroes and the challenge of humanity verses the infernal dieties. For the Aztecs the game was important in terms of the representation of the stars. Patolli, is a board game, similar to Parchessi. The board is in the form of a cross and the player must cover the board with 52 "houses." Fifty two is a significant number in the time cycle of the Aztecs. The game was played with "dice" or beans. The players "warmed" the beans for luck before throwing them, as we do today. They invoked the name of Macuiloxochitl, the diety of games, as they played the game. The Flying Pole game has now evolved into a dance and is performed on Corpus Christi Day.

Jai-alai is one of the most important games enjoyed by Mexicans today. This game, known as Frontón in Mexico, is played by two sides with anywhere from 1 to 3 players. They play on a court similar to handball called a "cancha," and are equipped with a leather glove attached to a long, curved wicker basket. The basket or "cesta," measures about 2 feet. Spectators sit along the side of the court behind a protective screen. The rubber ball may be hurled at speeds of up to 150 miles per hour. It can be an extremely fast and dangerous game. Jai-alai originated in the Basque region of France and Spain. Jai-alai means "merry festival" in basque.

Fútbol or soccer is a nationally played sport in Mexico. It's importance is equal to the place that soccer occupies in Europe as the largest spectator sport. The game is played by two opposing teams whose object is to score points by kicking or knocking the ball into a netted goal area. The ball may be hit with feet, knees, or the head, but never the hands. It is a game of stamina and endurance and is played on a large field over timed periods.

Sport Vocabulary

cancha   Jai-Alai court, similar to a handball court

corriente   common Mexican pottery for everyday use

deportes   sports

Flying Pole Dance   a daring dance performed by dancers on a high pole. Performed in Mexico on Corpus Cristi Day.

Frontón   the name for the game of Jai-Alai in Mexico. Jai-Alai is a fast ball game played on an indoor court, similar to handball.

Fútbol   the game of soccer

Huichol   Indians who live in Nyarit and produce beautiful wool textiles

lacquer   a process of creating intricately carved, painted objects

machete   Mexican knife with a long curved or straight blade

Macuiloxochitl   the Aztec god of games

maguey   Mexican plant whose fibers are used to make hammocks, mats and other products

peyote   cactus plant with hallucinogenic properties chewed by the Huichol

pinchanchas   pottery strainer for corn

patolli   ancient board game of chance

telar de otate   traditional Mexican loom used for weaving

Tlachtli   ancient ball game played on an enclosed court

Bullfighting

Bullfighting has been called a sport for many years which is probably a poor description because it is actually more like a drama, a demonstration or even a ballet. This presentation is far more dangerous than most others in that if the bullfighter makes a mistake, it may very well cost him his life.

Bullfighting is not really a duel between a man and a bull as it may seem; however, it is more of an art form and pageantry where a man conquers his fears and shows his bravery and skills to the applause and the admiration of all the spectators who watch.

It is also one of the few ways a poor man can become rich and, if he is particularly good, he could very well become a millionaire.

Bullfighting has been in existence for more than 2,000 years. The ancient Cretans performed bull dancing where other men and women leaped over the bulls in exhibitions.

The fighting bull first lived in Spain where Bullfighting originated. It is not the ordinary bull that is used but it is the "toro de lidia" or the "toro bravo" (brave bull) that has the special qualities for the bull arena. For many years, the wild bulls roamed throughout Spain. The Romans, around the 12th century, imported the bulls for the Colosseum to fight in the savage battles against man and beasts with the bulls usually the winners.

It was the Arabs in Spain that made bullfighting a popular event by killing the bull with a lance while on horseback. The common people used to help the nobles who were fighting the bulls by running, with capes, trying to distract the bull. This became the most popular part and it slowly developed into what it is today.

The bullfight was introduced to Mexico in 1526 to celebrate the return of Cortes from Honduras.

If you were to go to a bullfight, the first thing that you would see is the "plaza de Toros" (arena) filled with "aficionados" (fans). The music plays and the "toreros" parade around the stadium.

Everyone who fights the bull is called a "torero." The "matadores" are the central figures and there are usually only three each afternoon. Each "matador" has two "picadores" and three "banderilleros" to help him. The old term, "toreador" is seldom used any more.

The Matador chooses the bull he will fight and he watches the bull to see the way that he moves and especially how he throws his horns. These bulls are bred to fight and the minute the bull is in the ring, he knows that it is time for the battle.

After the original parade is over and the arena is cleared, the bull is released into the ring and the drama begins. A "banderillo" runs into the arena and swirls his cape in front of the bull to give the "matador" a chance to watch the bull and how he is reacting. The "banderillo" is awkward and not very graceful.

Soon, the matador enters the ring. He is graceful and lets the bull pass very close to him. He waves his cape smoothly and with the grace of a ballet dancer and the "aficionados" cheer. If he makes an awkward move, the crowds boo.

The bullfighter's cape is red on one side and yellow on the other. It is not the color of the cape that attracts the bull but it is the movement that lures the bull to attack the cape and not the body of the bullfighter.

After the "matador" does several passes, called "verónicas," a trumpet blows and the "picadores" enter on horseback. They prick the bull with their lances in order to weaken their neck muscles and to prevent the bull from charging with his head to the left or right. If they did not do this, it would be impossible for the matador to reach over the horns and place the sword blade between the bull's shoulder blades.

The next step further weakens the bull's neck muscles by placing two barbed sticks (banderillas) in the animal's shoulders by the "banderillos."

The "matador" re-enters the arena for the climax of the drama, the kill. He uses a little cape called the "muleta" and his sword. This is also the time of the greatest danger and the time when the life of a "matador" is in the balance.

The kill is also known as the "moment of truth" because it is at this very moment that decision is made between the bull and the bullfighter. The "matador" rushes at the bull at the same time the bull is charging the bullfighter and the "matador" must plunge the sword directly between the shoulder blades. If the bullfighter has done a good job, the bull will die instantly.

After the kill, the fans will cheer or boo depending on whether or not the fight was a good one in their eyes. The bull's ear will be awarded to the "matador" for a good fight but, if the fight was outstanding, the "matador" may receive the bull's two ears and his tail. The meat of the bulls is usually butchered in back of the stadium and sold as steaks. In some instances, the meat is given to the poor. There is a growing controversy over this custom—many people (including Mexicans) believe it to be inhumane.

Baseball

The people of the Yucatan Peninsula love the sport of baseball which is probably, a direct result of their ancestors. Almost every Maya ruin in Mexico and Central America has at least one court where the teams played a ball game that is not entirely understood today.

In the Mexican version, two stone rings protrude from opposite walls, and, it seems that the object of the game was to put the ball through one of the rings. Paintings on vases have shown that the hands could not be used and that only the hips and buttocks hits scored. The ball, evidently, was out of play or penalty points were given if it touched the ground.

Nevertheless, the game was very serious and had religious meanings as, perhaps, a battle between man and the gods. The loser of the game was often sacrificed.

The fact that it is indeed a sport of antiquity is proven in the fact that archeologists have discovered playing courts that date back to the sixth century B.C.

Children's Games

The native children of primitive communities today are, in all likelihood, playing the same games that their ancestors played since before the Conquest. Their parents either teach them or they learn by watching the grown-ups. Whatever they need to play with, they have to make themselves because either they do not have the money to buy them or they are not available. So the children learn early in life to amuse themselves.

Some of the games played with the children are very similar to those played today. This is as "This Little Pig Went to Market. . ."

El niño chiquito y bonito,
El señor de dos anillos,
El tonto y loco,
El lame cazuelas,
El mate piojos.

This little pretty child,
The master of the rings,
The foolish and crazy one,
The one that cleans the bowls,
The one that kills lice.

Este se robó un huevo
Este lo puso a asar,
Este le echó la sal,
Este lo comió,
Y este viejo perro le fué
      a chismear.

This one stole an egg,
This one fried it,
This one put salt on it,
This one ate it,
And this old dog went and
      tattled.

Muñecos de papel
(Paper Puppets)

Materials:
scissors, construction paper, white glue, string

Directions:
1. Cut circles, strips, triangles, squares of construction paper.

2. Use these to make a person or animal.

3. You may bend the paper or make rolls to make it more interesting.

4. Glue the pieces together and hang them from a string. Use your imagination.

The shapes in Spanish are:
circle	círculo
square	cuadrado
triangle	triángulo
rectangle	rectángulo

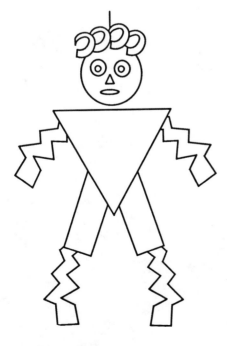

Juguetes de hierba
(Grass Toys)

Materials:
newsprint, drinking glass, grass seed, old blotter, paper, scissors, stapler, waterproof white glue, plant food.

Directions:
1. Plan a silhouette drawing of a person or animal on newsprint.

2. After you have found one you like, draw it again on the blotter paper.

3. Cut out your picture.

4. Glue grass seed to the back of your picture.

5. Staple another piece of blotter on back of drawing and let it hang into the glass of water.

6. Sprinkle with plant food and clip the grass occasionally.

Marionettes

Materials:
tag board or cardboard, scissors, crayons, metal fasteners

Directions:
1. Draw a picture of a person or animal with long necks, arms and legs.

2. Color and cut them out.

3. Cut off the legs, arms and head from the body.

4. Use fasteners to connect pieces.

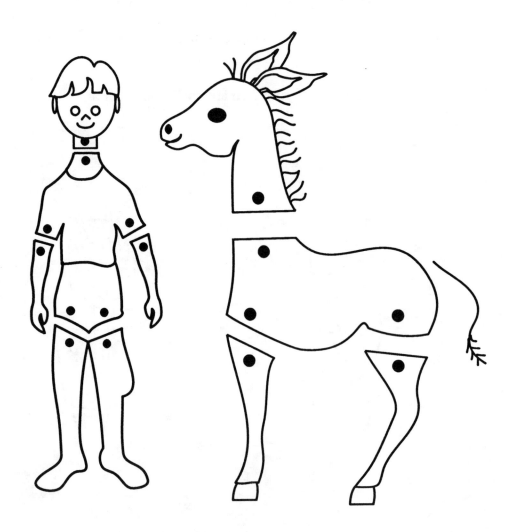

Hand Puppet I

Materials:
tag board (11" x 14"), tempera paint, brushes, scissors, metal fasteners

Directions:
1. Draw an animal or person, almost as large as the tag board.

2. Cut around the figure and paint it.

3. Cut two 1" bands for the back of the puppet.

4. Attach the two bands on the back of the puppet with the fasteners.

5. Be sure you have enough room to slide your hand in.

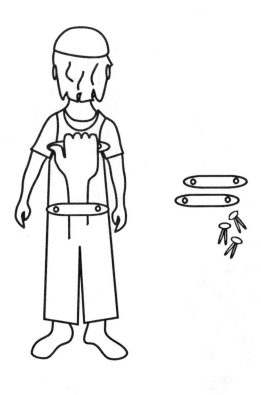 

Hand Puppet II

Materials:
paper bag, string, yarn, cotton, crepe paper, paint, crayons, brush

Directions:
1. Draw a face on upper half of the paper bag.

2. Stuff the top of the bag with crumpled paper, and tie a string around it to make the head.

3. Punch holes for the thumb and "pinkie" fingers.

4. Add string, yarn cotton or crepe paper for the details.

Handpuppet III

Materials:
sawdust, wallpaper paste, water, white glue, yarn, paper bag, tempera paint, brushes

Directions:
1. Mix one part paste with five parts sawdust. Mixture should be as thick as dough.

2. Shape a head and face. Make a hole for your finger.

3. Allow to dry.

4. Paint head, add features and glue on yarn as hair.

5. Attach a paper bag (upside down) for body.

Folded Paper Puppet

Materials:

paper

Directions:

1. Fold paper in half and then open.

2. Fold both the right and left edges in to meet the center fold.

3. Do not open.

4. Fold the right half over to the left side.

5. Fold bottom edge up to top edge. You now have two separate multi-layered flaps.

6. Put your fingers into the top pocket and the thumb in the bottom pocket. Draw a face using the inside fold as the mouth.

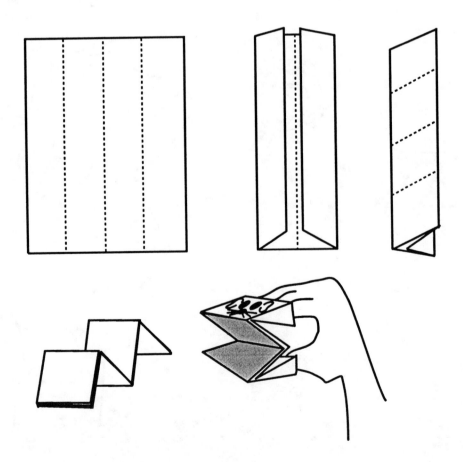

abril
APRIL

The
MAYAS

abril (April) Contents

April English/Spanish Vocabulary

animal   el animal, los animales

Conquerors   los conquistadores

earth   el mundo (world) la tierra (dirt)

endangered   en peligro

environment   el medioambiente

extinct   extinto

garbage   reciclar/to recycle,
       recursos naturales/natural resources

math   la matemática

Mayan   los Maya

monument   el monumental

plant   la planta (el arbusto/bush,
       el árbol/tree, bosque/forest)

trash   la basura

water   el agua

writing   la escritura (n.) escribir (to write)

Maya History

The Yucatán Peninsula of southeastern Mexico is a land that is as rich in history as it is in tradition. It was the center of the Mayan civilization which was in existence before the time of Columbus' discovery of the New World. Even today, a visitor can look across the dry, flat landscape and see an isolated, steep hill which is in all likelihood the ruin of a Mayan pyramid.

These monuments were usually built on sites that were directly related to the terrain. The peninsula, approximately 70,000 square miles, is basically made of limestone with few hills and virtually no rivers or streams that cross the land.

To compensate for this, the limestone absorbs the rain water which, in turn, dissolves the limestone which creates caves and channels and underground streams.

On the surface of the land, low oval basins called "aguadas" are formed which hold the water similar to a reservoir. These are known as cenotes and many are used for water wells.

In this dry land with little surface water, cenotes have long been used as a major source of water. The Mayans usually built very close to these cenotes or natural wells. They also used them for religious ceremonies such as at Chíchen-Ítza, the "virgins" were sacrificed and thrown into the cenotes.

The Maya began their long rise to a prominent civilization some 500 years before Christ was born. They reached a peak around A.D. 900, then they went into a decline that lasted until the last major Maya stronghold fell to the Spanish a little more than 300 years ago. But the Maya are still a people of the present world although they hang onto many of the customs of the past. The Mayan language is still spoken in remote corners of Guatemala and Belíze.

The Maya were farmers then, even as they are today. Nature, to them, was the key to survival. That is why their religion revolved around many gods that had to be appeased and honored to make sure the rains would fall and the crops would grow. The most important god of all was the rain god, Chac. Even today you can hear them say when it is raining, "Chac is falling."

The huts that the Mayans live in have not changed much since the time of the Mayans. The large pyramids were more ceremonial centers where the priests and kings lived.

Long before the Spanish conquistadores arrived (conquerors), the Maya had already abandoned their ceremonial centers and turned others into pure cities.

Some of the scholars suspect that the people began to balk at the priests' demands for human sacrifices. Others believe that since there is no evidence of the use of a wheel, that the people revolted against the hard labor and still others feel that the farmers killed the soil and burned the vegetation to clear the land and this off-set the balance of nature so that a drought occurred and the people began to starve.

The exact reason is still a mystery but new evidence is daily being uncovered and discovered through more knowledge in the interpretation of the Mayan writing and in new discoveries of pyramids and other ceremonial centers. We do know that the Spanish, in their zeal to convert the "pagans" to Christianity, burned and destroyed many artifacts and books and that the looters, in their desire to sell the Mayan artifacts, have destroyed many priceless monuments. Also, years have passed and the vegetation that is so thick and dense, have covered and preserved these ruins.

The Yucatan Peninsula today is a mixture of Mayan ruins, pyramids, and small pueblos to large cities such as Cancún where the shoreline is packed with over 140 luxury hotels. Although this is a major tourist attraction, it is said that 70 to 90 percent of the profits leave that area.

Yucatán Peninsula

The Maya prophet, Chilam Balam, predicted that men with beards would come from the east. They did just that beginning with the year 1517. The "conquest" started in Guatemala.

Francisco de Montejo gained permission from King Charles to conquer the peninsula at his own expense. It was so expensive and it was never completely successful.

The third invasion began at Can Perch – now Campecne – the oldest surviving European settlement in the Yucatán. The surrender took place at Ichansiho which is now Mérida, in 1542.

The Europeans were physically and emotionally remote in the Yucatán and they struggled for identity by declaring themselves a sovereign nation in 1840. They even hired the Texas navy to protect them from the Mayan guerrillas. In 1848, a delegation was sent to President Polk to apply for statehood.

Racism was a fact and way of life both in society and in business. At the top were the Spanish, born in Spain. Next, were the "criollos" – white, but born in Mexico. Farther down the ladder came the "mestizos" who were part white and part Indian; the "mulatos" which were part white and black; the "pardos" which were part black and Indian and, at the bottom, were the Indians.

The rejection of the Catholic Church by the new Mexican republic in 1847 until 1855 caused a Mayan uprising that ended with the massacre of entire towns by both sides.

Filling a spiritual vacuum, José María Barrera and a Maya ventriloquist named Manuel Hahuat created a "talking cross." The "cross" gathered thousands of followers know as "Cruzob" to the cult. Cruxob stood for "cruz" for cross in Spanish and "ob" for Maya plural suffix. The Cruzob ruled the area until they were overcome by the Mexican army in 1901.

Mayan Monuments

Calakmul may be the most massive pyramid that the Maya ever built at nearly 500 feet square and 175 feet high. From the top of this pyramid, it is possible to see the Dante pyramid at El Mirador some 23 miles away. El Mirador is the second largest pre-classic Maya city. Both pre-date Christ by a century. They both developed complex farming communities and complex political organizations. The cities flourished for a thousand years before a drought that may have forced them to abandon their city for, when the Spanish arrived, they only found around 600 people.

The most interesting part of the Maya is the fact that it is one civilization that is still currently being explored and new discoveries are being made on a regular basis.

This brilliant civilization that rose in the low-land jungle of the Yucatan Peninsula endured in cities that lasted until about A.D. 900 when some unexplained circumstances wrecked the delicate balance of what archeologists call the Classic period. One of the greatest Maya achievements was the most complex writing systems ever devised.

The Maya writing seems strange to us because we are used to our own system. They used what is called "glyph blocks." These may have been their sentences but instead of a line, they wrote in blocks. The blocks were arranged so they could be read left to right or right to left or, possibly, from top to bottom. The authorities feel that, although they are able to read many of the glyphs, they can only decipher about 30 percent.

Most of the blocks contain a dominant or main sign that fills most of the block. To this is added all the smaller elements. Until recently, it was thought that all the glyphs dealt only with the calendar and the gods. However, they have found the names of rulers and fragments of history.

In the 1560's the third bishop of Yucatán, wrote an accounting of the Mayas and although the original copy was lost, the Abbé de Bourbourgh found an abstract copy in the Madrid library in Spain. It contained a wonderful history of the Maya and their way of life along with a description of some of the workings of the calendar. It was complete in its description and drawings of the glyphs for "kin," or day and the names used for different days and months.

Beginning in 1880, Ernest Förstemann, the head librarian at Dresden, began to figure out the fundamental workings of the calendar. Förstemann had, at his disposal, the Postclassic Codex which was said to have been shipped to the then, Emperor Charles the V by Hernán Cortés.

Two main cycles were discovered; one of 260 days and one of 365 days. These sequences worked together as gear wheels. Each day was named in terms of both cycles, and the full name of any single day could repeat only every 18,980 days – once every 52 years.

To the Maya, the very days were gods, as were numbers. These moved relentlessly throughout eternity. Instead of a base-ten method such as ours, they used a base-twenty system to record dates.

The archeologists call these days "Long Count" dates and can relate them to our own calendar. Long Count dates record the number of days that have passed since the beginning of the Maya calendar – August 11, 3114 B.C. (February 11, A.D. 526 on our calendar).

A breakthrough came in 1959 when Tatiana Proskouriakoff discovered how to read the names of the emperors. This began the study of the political systems.

The Russian scholar Yuri Knorozov believes that, in addition to word signs, there are a number of glyphs that represent single syllables.

We do know that the Maya appeared from the depths of mystery and their civilizations left in the same way. During Europe's Dark Ages, the Maya practiced astronomy so precise that their ancient calendar was as accurate as the one we use today; they plotted celestial bodies and predicted solar and lunar eclipses. They calculated the course of Venus with an error of only 14 seconds a year. The Maya created a complex system of writing and initiated the mathematical concept of zero.

The Maya were far from being primitive farmers, they had very sophisticated methods of agriculture. They had fields capable of supporting large populations.

Throughout the various cities it has been found that there are variations in art, architecture, language and warfare and, yet, when the astronomers at Copán standardized the lunar calendar, it was quickly adopted throughout the Maya world indicating a communication between the cities.

Religion was the greatest unifying factor and the center of their civilization as seen by the great ceremonial centers of pyramids. Time also preoccupied their lives in terms that we may never understand. Their word "kin" means sun, day and time which blends the past and the present into one.

Human sacrifice outraged the Spaniards and they burned the Maya books and tore down the pyramids and used the stones to build their own structures. The Mayas converted but not completely as they did not give up their deities entirely and often combined the Christian and Maya traditions in their celebrations and lives. For example, if weeds grow in the corn field, the souls of the corn plants will move to cleaner fields.

Now, only the ruins remain. The "Children of Time" knew that all of this would happen for one of their prophets wrote: "All moons, all years, all days, all winds, take their course and pass away."

Environmental Activities

One of the possible causes of the demise of the Maya people is that the farmers slashed and burned the rain forest to create fields for their crops. The ground will only grow three crops of corn before another field has to be located which would also cause the farmer to destroy other land.

The destruction of the rain forest plus the lack of rivers and streams could have caused a drought that caused the crops to die and hunger set in.

The same type of condition is happening today in Mexico, Guatemala and other countries. It is an opportune time to study these conditions and to put ecology into your curriculum. For example:

1. Study the effect the 900 mile Amazonia highway is having in Brazil.

2. Study the effect of the destruction of the rain-forest and the "greenhouse effect."

3. Study the endangered species that have occurred in animals because of the destruction of their habitats.

4. Discuss and study the role of litter and water pollution and the animals and plants in the forest.

5. Study "Earth Day" and its meaning.

6. Earth Day or environmental Activities/Information:

The Celebration of the Outdoors
1250 24th Street NW, Suite 500
Washington, DC 20460

The National Arbor Day Foundation
100 Arbor Avenue
Nebraska City, NE 68410

Keep America Beautiful, Inc.
Mill River Plaza
9 W Broad Street
Stamford, CT 06902

PBS Elementary/Secondary
Services-Dept. PR
1320 Braddock Place
Alexandria, VA 22314

National Wildlife Federation
(check your phone book)

Acid Rain

Acid Rain Test

Materials:
   small cup
   antacid tablet containing calcium carbonate
   tablespoon
   white vinegar

Directions:
1. Put the antacid tablet inside a see-through cup. The tablet contains calcium carbonate. The pyramids are made of stones that contain calcium carbonate.

2. Pour one tablespoon of vinegar (a mild acid) over the tablet. What happened? Are there bubbles? What is happening to the tablet?

3. Now, put the cup in a place where it will get direct sunlight. Check it and make observations everyday for three days. Record your findings if you want.

4. What happened to the acid? What happened to the tablet? (You should have a white powder remaining.)

5. In what way is acid rain like vinegar?

6. What effect do you think the acid rain is making on the pyramids?

What Can Kids Do To Protect the Atmosphere?

1. Encourage parents to buy products that are not in an aerosol can. Take an aerosol can survey on hair spray of the homes. Have the children talk to their parents about the importance of not using aerosols. How many can each child find in the home?

2. Talk about smog and cars. How many children's parents have had to have smog checks done on their cars?

Litter/Recycling

The Recycling Room

Be the classroom where recycling begins! How can this happen?

1. Save and reuse paper that is not fully used.

2. Set up recycling centers in your room for not only your room but for the whole school.

3. Encourage the children to use the lunch bag they used for lunch again.

4. Have the children encourage their parents to buy products that can be recycled; for example, washing detergent can be bought in boxes instead of plastic bottles. How many more products can you think of? (milk, fabric softener etc.)

5. Examine a child's lunch from home. Discuss what can be recycled and what cannot. What can be thrown away and what cannot? What could you change to make less garbage? (an example might be a thermos instead of another drink, lunch pail instead of a paper bag, reusable hard plastic container for food etc.)

6. Take a "junk" walk and gather all the trash and make new "inventions" or "creations" with the trash in the classroom.

7. Collect aluminum cans in your classroom and have each child save the tab as a point or a cent. Have the children donate their old toys and have a "sale" and the children can use their tabs or "points" to buy. With the money from the sale of the cans, buy a tree for the school or local park.

8. Post the slogan "If you see it, pick it up." Discuss this slogan in regards to litter. Ask the principal if your class could pick up trash one day or one week. Display the amount of litter found for the school to see.

Water

Brainstorm the class to see how many different things they know that would pollute the water. (dumping of wastes, people littering, oil spills, run-offs etc.) Then, discuss the results of water pollution on the animals, people, plants etc.

Fill a one-gallon jar with water three-fourths full. Make two peep holes in a piece of black construction so that when you wrap it around the jar, the two holes are opposite from each other. Secure the paper with tape. Shine a flashlight through the jar by pointing it through the peep holes. Hold up another sheet of black construction paper behind the jar to catch the beam of light. The children should see the light shinning brightly. Add several handfuls of dirt to the water and shake it up. Keep the dirt suspended in the water and shine the light again. The light should be dimmer. Continue with the dirt.

Through this experiment, the children should recognize the fact that plants and animals living in the water cannot live without the sunlight that comes through the water. If that light is blocked, they cannot survive.

What Can Kids Do?

1. Be a water saver at home and at school! Discuss the ways that someone can save water. Fix leaks and drips, turn off the water when brushing your teeth, rinse the dishes all at once, take a shorter shower and a shower instead of a bath.

2. Children can be encouraged to talk to the parents to help conserve water by not over watering their lawns, doing small loads of laundry, etc. Have the children discover ways.

3. Do not throw litter by the rivers or lakes. Discuss how litter not only harms the water but also the animals.

Endangered Plants and Animals

Imagine! The quetzal bird that is such an important part of Mexico's history is a threatened bird because of the pollution and destruction of the rain forest where he finds his home. He is not alone.

In 1950, one-fourth of the world was covered with forests. In 1980, one-fifth of those forests were cut down. The biggest losses are in the rain forest. What can be done?

1. Your class could write letters to encourage the passage of legislation to save and protect the forests.

2. If your school is near a forest, raise money or just volunteer to plant trees instead of a field-trip for fun.

3. Plant flowers at your school or make a pocket garden in a neglected area that needs brightening up.

4. Make bird feeders for food and water as an art activity. Encourage the children to use them at home.

5. Learn about the endangered species and study ways to help them.

6. Do not buy products that come from endangered species and ask the children to explain these to their parents and ask for their help too.

7. Talk about the child's pet and how they care for it. Enlarge on that with other animals.

8. Find a better way to celebrate than to release helium balloons. Animals find the balloons and since they do not decay, they often eat them.

9. Pick up litter that might hurt an animal. (Good idea just to pick it up anyway.)

Maya Math

The wheels of time to the Maya were very exact. They were basically used to predict the seasons for the farmers and the astronomical events for the religious rites. For this they used a calendar of two meshings thereby repeating cycles. Maya mathematicians could project this calendar millions of years into the future and the future; therefore, time had no beginning or end.

The Maya used a system of bars and dots. A dot equals one and a bar equals five. The smaller wheels represented the 260-day Sacred Round. The inner wheel, with the numbers one to thirteen, meshes with the glyphs for the 20 day name on the outer wheel which represents the 365-day calendar — 18 months of 20 days each. The remaining five days at the end of the year were considered evil.

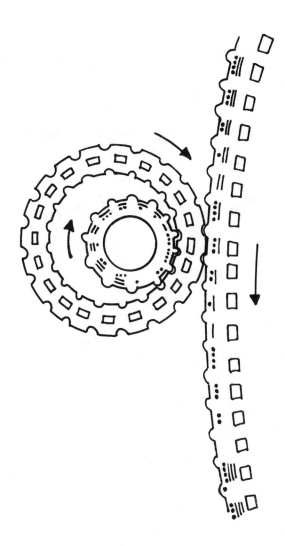

Mayan Arithmetic

Long ago in Mexico and Central America, the Maya lived and they had a very interesting way of writing numbers:

For zero they used a shell.　　⊝

For one they used a dot.　　•

For five they used a line.　　——

By using only the dot, the line and the shell, they were able to write all the existing counting numbers.

one •　　three •••　　five ——　　eight •••	(underlined)　　ten ══

Below are some examples of how you can use Mayan Arithmetic.

What would the Mayans write for:

4?　　　　　　　6?　　　　　　　nine?

How would you write the answers in Mayan Arithmetic?

4 + 2 =　　　　　8 - 5 =　　　　　4 x 2 =

Maya Dig

1. Out of clay, design and make your own artifacts.

2. In a designated area in a vacant lot or in a sandbox have your own archeological dig.

3. Include a "treasure" or designate one artifact for the "find" of the day.

4. Did you find them all?

mayo

MAY

Cinco De Mayo
Revolución
Música
CINCO DE MAYO
REVOLUTION
MUSIC

mayo (May) Contents

Vocabulary for May

bandit	el bandido
bell	la campana
drum	el tambor, timpano
flute	la flauta
guitar	la guitarra
house	la casa
keyboard	teclado
music	la música
musical note, clef	clave
piano	piano
to play	tocar
president	el presidente
revolution	la revolución
saxophone	el saxófono
trumpet	la trompeta
tuba	tuba
violin	violín

History of Cinco De Mayo

The revolts of the early nineteenth century led by Hidalgo and Morelos were directed against the power that Spain and the church held over the Indian and Mestizo. These events led to the Independence of Mexico from Spain in 1814. Nevertheless, the wealth of the country was still concentrated in the hands of a few individuals and the Indian population was subject to abuses from government officials and the church.

During the 1840's, Benito Juárez, a Zapotec Indian began his political work in Oaxaca. Juárez became governor in 1847, but was exiled to New Orleans in 1853 because of his statements about the corrupt activities of General Santa Anna and the need for reform. He is known as the "Abraham Lincoln of Mexico" because of his commitment to equality for all Mexicans. In 1861, Benito triumphantly returned to Mexico as President, to institute the Constitution of 1857 and the laws which removed special privileges and political power from the hands of the church.

One of Benito Juárez' first actions as President was to suspend the interest payments on foreign debts. This angered the European powers, and France saw this as an opportunity to intervene. Napoleon III hoped to be able to control all of Mexico and the liberal forces of Juárez. French forces occupied Veracruz by the end of 1861. On May 5, 1862, General Zaragoza and his Mexican forces defeated the French in a battle at Puebla. This battle has come to symbolize the strength and determination of the Mexican people and is celebrated every year as Cinco de Mayo.

After the death of Benito Juárez in 1877, General Porfirio Díaz, who had made several attempts at the Presidency, conducted another revolt. He successfully became President in 1880. He ruled as a dictator, and although he made many economic and commercial advances, he had little regard for the poor. He acknowledged the landowners and the church and kept their favor by increasing their wealth and privilege. A spirit of unrest grew among the people.

In 1910, Díaz allowed the liberal party in Mexico to put forward an opposition candidate. The person chosen was Francisco Madero. He was popular among the people, and although he was imprisoned for a time by Díaz, he became a force for revolutionary change. Unfortunately, he was unable to keep power when he was elected President in 1911 and a succession of other rebel leaders followed including; Emiliano Zapata and Pancho Villa. Victoriano Huerta seized control of the government in 1913 and ruled as dictator after he had Madero murdered. Revolts led by Zapata, Villa, and Venustiano Carranza continued to break out in the country.

In 1915 a special commission, representing 8 Latin American countries and the U.S., officially recognized Carranza as President. The rebel leaders laid down their arms, with the exception of Villa. In 1917, a new constitution provided for reforms in land distribution, labor, political office, and church privileges. Carranza was unable to enforce many of the reforms called for in the constitution, the unrest continued, and Carranza was killed in a revolt by Huerta in 1920.

The Revolutionary period, while a time of turmoil and hardship, also produced some of Mexico's greatest leaders and legends. The "corridos" or ballads of this era have preserved the fascinating stories of the people who lived through this era of Mexican history.

History & Legend of Pancho Villa

The History

Pancho Villa is one of the most controversial figures in the history of Mexico. The questions always arise as to whether he was a bandit, traitor, murderer, Robin Hood, heroic general or a man to be honored. History shows us that he was a man to be feared and the legend behind Pancho Villa explains the possible reason for it is said that he sold his soul to the devil.

Pancho was the illegitimate son of a rich hacendado (owner of a hacienda) in the state of Durango. His father would not acknowledge him as his son, so his mother gave him to a peasant whom he called abuelo (grandfather). As the boy roamed the hills and as he worked in the fields, he learned about people and animals. He attended eight days of school in his life.

Doroteo Arango was Pancho's given name that he used for the first twenty years of his life. He was physically strong, fearless and cruel and he learned to gamble and steal at an early age. Once he was caught by the police and sentenced to death but someone interceded for him and he was released provided that he become a soldier and join in the squelching of an uprising of the natives of Los Mochis. During that time, one of the bravest soldiers named Francisco Villa was killed and, so to keep his memory alive, Doroteo assumed his name and he became Francisco Villa with the nickname "Pancho."

Villa began as a simple soldier in the Maderistas in 1910 and fought on the side of the people but soon gained prestige in the ranks. He surrounded himself with a group of daredevils called Los Dorados who were willing to follow Pancho everywhere or to do anything.

As he became more well-known, some of the most refined and cultured Mexican revolutionaries joined his following.

In 1920 when General Alvaro became president, Pancho Villa surrendered saying, "From now on I do not wish to kill anymore of my brothers. I want to be an honorable man and to serve my country in another form. Come boys, let us go to Canutillo to till the soil." This was not to be for in 1923, Pancho Villa was assassinated and no one knows by whom.

However, Pancho Villa still lives in the hearts of the people for he loved them and was always kind to the poor and was ready to listen to them. To the people, Villa was a supernatural being who thought nothing of killing for the sport. He was both good and evil. Maybe the legend will explain.

The Legend

In the North of San Juan del Río there is an iron mountain shaped like a coffin where the young men of the region of Durango go when they reach puberty. Legend says that when these young men return, they are completely transformed. The reason is, the old women say, that the mountain is full of wizards or sorcerers and even the devil himself. The young men trade their souls for power, wisdom or whatever their dreams entail and this is understandable in the eyes of the Mexicans in this part of the country. Durango boasted of the best gamblers, the most daring horsemen, passionate lovers, invincible fighters and the most prosperous merchants.

Knowing that all this could be his, Doroteo stole a horse in the middle of the night, it is said, and went in search of this mountain shaped like a coffin filled with creatures who could turn him from a boy into a man.

Looking for the rock that covered the entrance, he searched. A rattlesnake slithered by and seemed to disappear into the rocks. It was the entrance. Doroteo followed the snake which led him through a cavern and a path that led to the very heart of the mountain. The walls were filled with veins of silver and gold but even the great riches could not keep him from continuing down the path. He turned a corner and suddenly there was a great light, a volcanic center, a voice rang out, deep and sinister asking why Doroteo was there. Doroteo was very calm for he knew what he wanted and was not afraid to ask. " I want to to be a man ... an exceptional man."

El Diablo (the devil) was willing to give more. He offered Doroteo the opportunity to become a historic person – loved and hated by many, revered and feared by others. For a price, Doroteo would become Francisco Villa or Pancho Villa, a name that would be known around the world. No longer a child but a man so dangerous that he would be famous for his daring and fearless feats.

Doroteo was eager to agree. What was the price? First, Doroteo had to give up forever, all that is holy. He had to defy the Virgin and God. The second? One minute after death, Doroteo's soul would belong to El Diablo.

As Pancho Villa left the cavern, it is said that his soul could be seen in the corner weeping.

History has proven that indeed, Pancho Villa was one of the most dangerous of them all. He truly was an exceptional man.

Music

Ancient music in Mexico was usually created with drums, wind instruments, and the human voice. Music was used as part of religious, military or community ceremonies. There are two kinds of pre-conquest drums still in use today. One is the Aztec *huehuetl*, which is tall and round. The second is the *teponaxtli*, also round but horizontal. Reed or clay flutes called *chirimias* were played by Indians long before the conquest and are still creating their exotic sounds for modern Mexico. Shells, bones, and gourds were also used for early instruments and continue in many areas today. Stringed instruments made from the shell of the armadillo are an example of this type of instrument. Whatever the instrument, ancient music often sought to imitate the sounds of nature and invoke a feeling of unity. When ancient Aztec warriors went on a journey alone, they often brought an instrument with them to help them on their way.

The conquest of Mexico by the Spaniards brought the influence of new instruments, a new rhythm and, as in other areas of Indian life, Spanish music was incorporated into the native culture. Today one can hear a great variety of music in Mexico. The Deer Dance of the Yaqui Indians maintains the traditional indigenous sounds of the gourd rattles (sonajas) and the raspadores (wooden rasps).

The Mariachi bands, so popular in Mexico today, originated in Spain. A strolling folk orchestra, they originally only played stringed instruments; the guitar, guitarrón (like a large guitar), violin, and vibuela (viola). Cornets and trumpets were added later and are now usually seen as part of the group. The Mariachis begin each performance with a "sinfonía" or little tune played before the song and repeated between verses. At first only men played but today there are women Mariachis as well. The French emperor, Maximillian, enjoyed the music of the Mexican bands and often asked the groups to play at the weddings of his friends. The word "mariage" means marriage in French, hence the Spanish adaptation "mariachi".

The "Corrido" or ballad, developed during the revolutionary period (1910-1920). The corridos generally consist of the same musical repetition, but the words change to tell stories of great adventures, heroes, and love. They have always been music for the "people." Publishing houses produced the inexpensive sheet music, folksingers learned the notes, but were often illiterate so changed the words to fit the story they remembered. Corridos about current events or politics are soon forgotten. But corridos which appeal to the emotions live on. Lucia or Adelita are examples. These songs were a comfort to soldiers during the revolution who had to face hardship, death, and a life away from the warmth of home and family.

Mexican Maracas

Paper Mache

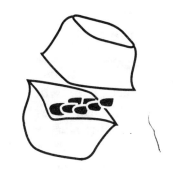

1. Carefully cut the portion of the egg carton that holds the eggs from the whole carton.

2. Put some stones, popcorn (not popped) or dry, hard objects that will make noise, into the cartons.

3. Poke a hole in the bottom of one of the cartons and put a stick or pencil in the hole for the handle.

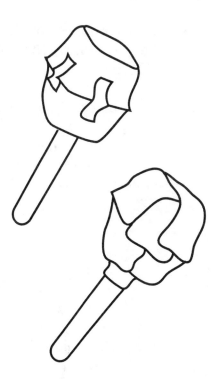

4. Tape the two pieces of the carton together.

5. Using newspaper strips, dip them into wheat paste or liquid starch and cover the cartons together making sure that the stick is anchored into the cartons.

6. Let the maraca dry.

7. Now, paint your maraca bright colors with Mexican designs and you are ready to play.

From *MEXICAN*, by Barbara Schubert and Marlene Bird.
Copyright © 1976. A Reflections & Images Publication.
San Jose, California. Reprinted with permission.

Light Bulb Maracas

1. You will need to save your light bulbs for this project.

2. Apply strips of newspaper dipped in liquid starch or wheat paste to a burned out light bulb. Be sure to apply several coats for you will need the strength of the paper.

3. Let your maraca dry, thoroughly.

4. Hit the maraca on a table or the floor to break the glass inside the bulb. Be careful that the children do not hit them too hard.

5. Patch holes, if need be and dry again.

6. If there are no holes and the maraca is ready, paint it and you will find that the broken glass makes the noise inside the maraca.

Drums

The easiest way to make a drum is to simply use a Quakers Oat box with the lid or a coffee can, again with the lid.

1. Cut a piece of construction paper the height of the drum base and enough wider so that it can be glued.

2. Draw, paint or color a design on the paper and cut it out.

3. Glue the paper to the drum base (the can or box) and you are ready to join the band!

Corrido De Lucio

Ballad of Lucio

A las once de la noche
estaba Lucio cenando,
cuando legan sus amigos
y lo invitan al fandango.

Su madre se lo decía
que a ese fandango no fuera;
los consejos de una madre,
no se llevan como quiera.

Lo sacaron a la orilla
por ver si sabía jugar;
tres puñaladas le dieron
al pie de un verde nopal.

Su hermano de compasión,
la pistola le brindó;
"Ora para que la quiero,
si ya la hora pasó."

Madre mía de Guadalupe,
de Villa de Jerez,
dame la licencia, Senora,
de levantarme otra vez.

Su pobre madre lloraba,
pase~ándose en los portales;
"¿Cómo quieres levantarme
si son heridas mortales?"

Coro:
Santo Niñito de Atocha,
deVilla de Jerez,
dame licencia, Niñito,
de levantarme vez.

Vuela, vuela, palomita,
avisa a toda la gente,
que no sigan el ejemplo
del hijo desobediente.

At eleven o'clock at night
Lucio was eating supper,
When his friends came
And invited him to the fandango.

His mother told him
Not to go to that fandango;
The advice of a mother
Cannot be taken lightly.

They took him aside
To see if he knew how to play;
They gave him three stabs
At the foot of the green nopal.

His brother out of pity
Offered him his pistol.
"Now, what do I want it for,
It is too late."

Mother mine of Guadalupe,
From the Villa of Jerez,
Give me leave Senora,
To get up again.

His poor mother wept,
Pacing in the entrance
"How can you want me to get up;
These wounds are mortal."

Chorus:
Holy child of Atocha,
From the Villa of Jerez,
Give me leave, little one,
To get up again.

Fly, fly, little dove,
Tell all the people,
Not to follow the example,
Of the disobedient son.

Adelita

This is the most famous of all the corridos from the Revolución.

En lo alto de una abrupta serranía
donde estaba y acampado un regimiento,
una joven que valiente los seguía
porque estaba enamorada de un
    sargento.

Popular entre la tropa era Adelita,
la mujer por el sargento idolatrada
porque a más de ser valiente era
bonita
Y hasta el mismo coronel la res-
    petaba.

Y se cuenta que decía él cuánto
    la quería:

Si Adelita se fuera con otro
le siguiría las huellas sin cesar,
si por mar en un buque de guerra,
si por tierra en un tren militar.

Si Adelita ha de ser mi esposa,
si Adelita ha de ser mi mujer,
Adelita, Adelita del alma,
Adelita de mi corazón.

Si Adelita quisiera ser mi esposa,
si Adelita fuera mi mujer
le compraría un vestido de seda,
para llevarla a bailar el cuartel.

Adelita, por Dios te lo ruego,
calma el fuego de esta mi pasión,
porque te amo y te quiero rendido
y por tí sufre mi fiel corazón.

Si Adelita se fuera con otro,
le seguiría la huella sin cesar,
si por mar, en un buque de guerra,
si por tierra, en tren militar.

On the heights of an abrupt ridge,
Where a regiment was camping.
A valiant young girl followed it
Because she was in love with a
    sergeant.

Favorite among the troop was
    Adelita,
The woman idolized by the
    sergeant,
Because being brave, she was pretty.
And even the Colonel respected her.

And it is related that he said
    how much he loved her.

If Adelita were to go with another,
He would follow her tracks with-
    out rest;
If by sea, in a war boat,
If by land, a military train.

Yes, Adelita must be my wife,
Yes, Adelita must be my woman.
Adelita, Adelita of my soul,
Adelita of my heart.

If Adelita wanted to be my wife,
If Adelita were my woman
I would buy her a silk dress,
To take her to dance at the
    barracks.

Adelita, for God's sake I beg you
To calm the fire of this passion,
Because I adore you and love
    you, devotedly
And you you my faithful heart suffers.

Toca el clarín de campaña a la
    guerra,
sale el valiente guerrero a pelear,
correrían los arroyos de sangre,
¡Qué gobierne un tirano jamás!

Y si acaso yo muero en campaña
y mi cuerpo en la sierra va a
    quedar,
Adelita, por Dios te lo ruega,
con tus ojos me vas a llorar.
En lo alto de una abrupta serranía

Here the first verse is repeated which is the
refrain.

The bugle of battle plays to war,
The brave knight leaves to fight.
Streams of blood shall flow,
Let no tyrant ever govern!

And if perchance I die in battle
And if my body remains in the
    sierra,
Adelita, for God's sake I beg you,
To weep for me with your eyes,
On the heights of an abrupt ridge.

Adelita

En lo alto de uña a - brup - ta se - rra - ni

a donde es - taba ya a - cam pa - do un re - gi - mien-

to un - a jo - ven que va lien - te los se gui

a por - que es - taba e - namo - ra - da de un sargen-

to Po - pu - lar - en tre - la tro - pa era Ad - li-

ta la mu - jer por el sar - gen - to ido - la tra-

da por - que a más de ser va - lien te era bo - ni-

ta yhasta - el mis mo co - ro nel la res - pe

ta - ba____ y se cuen - ta____ que de

Adelita

di - a_____ él cuan - la que - ri - a   Si A - de-
li - ta se fue - ra con o - tro le se - qüi-
rí - a las hue - llas sin - cer_____ si por
mar en un bu - que de gue - rra_____ Si - por
tie - rra en un tren mi - li - tar_____ Si A - del
li - ta ha de ser mi es - po - sa_____ Si A - de
li - ta ha de ser mi mu - jer_____ A - de-
li - ta A de - li - ta del al - ma_____ A - de-

1.
li - ta de mi - cor - a - zón_____ A - de-

2.
zón

La Cucaracha

This is a very popular revolutionary song that is from Chihuahua. It begins with the chorus, which is sung after every verse. This song can go on forever for each singer is to make up his own verses.

Coro:
La cucaracha, la cucaracha
ya no puede caminar
porque no tiene, porque le falta
limonada que tomar.

Chorus:
The cockroach, the cockroach
Can no longer walk,
Because he hasn't, because he hasn't,
lemonade to drink.

Ya murío la cucaracha,
ya la llevan a enterrar
entre cuatro zopilotes
y un ratón de sacristan.

The cockroach is now dead
And is taken to be buried
Between four buzzards
And a rat of a Sacristan.

Con las barbas de Carranza,
voy a hacer una toquilla,
pa' ponérsela al sombrero
de su padre Pancho Villa.

With the whiskers of Carranza,
I'm going to make a hat band,
To put it on the sombrero
Of his father Pancho Villa.

Un panadero fué misa,
no encontrando qué rezar,
le pidió a la Virgin pura,
limonada que tomar.

A baker went to mass,
Not finding anything to pray for,
He asked the pure Virgin,
For lemonade to drink.

Una cosa me da risa:
Pancho Villa sin camisa;
ya se van los carrancistas
porque vienen los villistas.

One thing makes me laugh,
Pancho Villa in his shirt;
Now the Carranzistas are leaving,
Because the Villistas are coming.

Para sarapes Saltillo,
Chihuahua para soldados;
para mujeres, Jalisco;
para amar, todito lados.

For serapes, Saltillo,
Chihuahua, for soldiers;
For women, Jalisco;
For love, everywhere!

La Cucaracha

Jarabe Tapatio
(Mexican Hat Dance)

T.S. Denison & Co., Inc.

260

Canciones para Aprender
(Learning Songs)

¿Qué Comer?
What To Eat?
(Tune of "Brother John")

Hoy es lunes,
Hoy es lunes,
¿Qué comer?
¿Qué comer?
Lunes los ejotes.
Lunes los ejotes.
M-m-m, M-m-m.

Hoy es martes,
Hoy es martes,
¿Qué comer?
¿Qué comer?
Lunes los ejotes,
Martes los camotes.
M-m-m, M-m-m.

Hoy es miércoles,
Hoy es miércoles,
¿Qué comer?
¿Qué comer?
Martes los camotes,
Miércoles las fresas.
M-m-m, M-m-m.

Hoy es jueves,
Hoy es jueves,
¿Qué comer?
¿Qué comer?
Miércoles las fresas,
Jueves las cerezas.
M-m-m, M-m-m.

Today is Monday,
Today is Monday,
What to eat?
What to eat?
Monday, the green beans,
Monday, the green beans,
M-m-m, M-m-m.

Today is Tuesday,
Today is Tuesday,
What to eat?
What to eat?
Monday, the green beans,
Tuesday, the sweet potatoes,
M-m-m, M-m-m.

Today is Wednesday,
Today is Wednesday,
What to eat?
What to eat?
Tuesday, the sweet potatoes,
Wednesday, the strawberries,
M-m-m, M-m-m.

Today is Thursday,
Today is Thursday,
What to eat?
What to eat?
Wednesday, the strawberries
Thursday, the cherries,
M-m-m, M-m-m.

Hoy es viernes,
Hoy es viernes,
¿Qué comer?
¿Qué comer?
Jueves las cerezas,
Viernes el pescado.
M-m-m, M-m-m.

Hoy es sábado,
Hoy es sábado,
¿Qué comer?
¿Qué comer?
Viernes el pescado,
Sábado helado.
M-m-m, M-m-m.

Hoy es domingo,
Hoy es domingo.
¿Qué comer?
¿Qué comer?
Algo hay de todo,
Y de este modo,
Lunes los ejotes,
Martes los camotes,
Miércoles las fresas,
Jueves las cerezas,
Viernes el pescado,
Sábado helado.
¡Ay de mí! ¡Ay de mí!

Today is Friday,
Today is Friday,
What to eat?
What to eat?
Thursday, the cherries,
Friday, the fish.
M-m-m, M-m-m.

Today is Saturday,
Today is Saturday,
What to eat?
What to eat?
Friday, the fish,
Saturday ice cream.
M-m-m, M-m-m.

Today is Sunday,
Today is Sunday,
What to eat?
What to eat?
Something of everything
And in this order.
Monday, the green beans,
Tuesday, the sweet potatoes,
Wednesday, the strawberries, Thurs-
day, the cherries,
Friday, the fish,
Saturday ice cream.
¡Ay de mi! ¡Ay de mi!

Los Días de la Semana
The Days of the Week
(Tune of Twinkle, Twinkle, Little Star)

Lunes, martes, miércoles, tres, jueves, viernes, sábado, seis; domingo siete, y
sabe ya que la semana pasada completa está.

La marcha de las letras
The March of the Letters

Que dejen toditos los libros abiertos
Ha sido la orden que dio el general,
Que todos los niños estén muy atentos,
Las cinco vocales van a desfilar.

Primero verán que pasa la A
Con sus dos patitas muy abiertas al marchar.
Ahí viene la E, alzando los pies.
El palo del medio es más chico como ven.
Aquí está la I, la sigue la O:
Una es flaca y otra gorda porque ya comió.
Y luego hasta atrás llegó U
Como la cuerda con que siempre saltas tú.
inglés:

Leave the books open, ordered
the general.
All the children are attentive,
The vowels are going to march.

First you all will see the A pass
With his two feet open to march.
Here come the E, lifting the feet,
The middle stick is the shortest you'll see.
Here is the I, the O follows:
One is skinny and the other fat because he's already eaten.
And then behind came the U
Like the rope with which you always jump.
(This rhyme is often heard as the children jump rope.)

Treinta Días Tiene septiembre
Thirty Days Has September

Treinta días tiene septiembre,
abril, junio y noviembre;
febrero tiene veíntiocho,
y los demás treinta y uno.

Colores
Colors
(Tune of "La Raspa")

Este mi canto es
colores que puedo ver;
los nombres aprender
así lo voya hacer . . .
rojo, azul, verde, amarillo
anaranjado, cafe y morado
negro y blanco son diferentes.
¿Cuántos colores te he mencionado?
(nueve)

This my song will be
Of colors that I may see;
The names I need to know
I'll have to learn them so . . .
Red and blue, green and yellow,
Orange, brown and purple, too,
Black and white are not alike
How many colors have I mentioned?
(nine)

Los Pollitos
The Chicks

Los pollitos dicen -pío, pío, pío-,
Cuando tienen hambre,
Cuando tienen frío.
La gallina busca el maíz y
    el trigo.
Les da la comida,
Y les presta abrigo.
Acurrucaditos bajo las dos alas,
Hasta el otro día duermen los
    pollitos.

The little chicks say, "peep,
    peep, peep"
When they are hungry,
When they are cold.
The hen looks for corn and wheat.
She gives them food,
And she keeps them warm.
Huddling them under her wings,
They sleep until the next day.

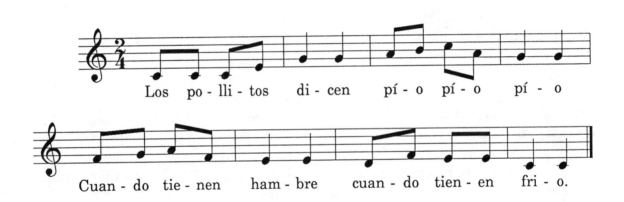

Los po - lli - tos di - cen pí - o pí - o pí - o

Cuan - do tie - nen ham - bre cuan - do tien - en fri - o.

Mi Rancho
My Farm

Vengan a ver mi rancho que es hermoso
Vengan a ver mi rancho que es hermoso.
El perrito hace así: guau, guau,
El perrito hace así: guau, guau.
O ven camarada, o ven camarada,
O ven, o ven, o ven,
o ven camarad, o ven camarad,
o ven o ven, o ven.
(otros hacen así. . .)   el patito hace así: cua, cua . . .
                           el gatito hace así: miau, miau . . .
                           el burro hace así: ji-jo, ji-jo.

Come to see my farm (ranch) that is beautiful
The dog says: woof, woof.
Oh, come friend, oh come friend,
Oh, come, oh come, oh come.
(others say . . .)   the duck says quack. . .
                       the cat says meow. . .
                       the burrow says hee-haw.

Mi Rancho

Ven-gan-a ver-mi ran-cho que es her-mos-o

Ven-gan a ver-mi ran-cho que es her-mo-so

El pe-rri-to hace-a-sí guau-guau

El per-ri-to hace a-sí guau-guau O

ven cam-a-rad O ven ca-ma-rad O ven, O ven O ven O

ven cam-a rad O ven ca-ma-rad O ven o ven o ven

Lullaby

Duér-mase mi niño que ten-go que ha-cer
Qué-el diá de su santo se la ha de poner

un-a cam i-si-ta que le voy ha-cer.
a la ru ru ru a la re re re.

La Rana
This song is the equivalent to
"The House that Jack Built"

Estaba la rana cantando debajo del
   agua,
cuando la araña se puso a cantar,
vino la mosca y la hizo callar.

Callaba la mosca la rana
que estaba cantando debajo del
   agua;
cuando la mosca se puso a cantar,
vino la araña y la hizo callar.

Callaba la araña a la mosca, la
   mosca a la rana
que estaba cantando debajo del
   agua;
cuando la araña se puso a cantar,
vino el ratón y la hizo callar.

Callaba el hombre al cuchillo, el
   chuchillo al toro, el toro al agua,
el agua al fuego, el fuego al palo, el
   palo al perro,
el perro al gato, el gato al ratón, el
   ratón a la arana,
la arana a la mosca, la mosca a la
   rana
que estaba cantando debajo del agua;
cuando el hombre se puso a cantar;
vino su suegra y lo hizo callar.

The frog was singing under the
   water,
When the spider began to sing,
Came the fly and made her shut up.

The fly made the frog shut up,
Who was singing under the
   water;
When the fly began to sing,
Came the spider and made her
   shut up.

The spider shut the fly up,
   the fly the frog
Winging under the water;
When the spider began to sing
Came the mouse and shut it up.

The man shut the knife up, the
   knife the bull, the bull the water,
The water the fire, the fire, the
   stick, the stick the dog,
The dog the cat, the cat the mouse,
the mouse the spider,
The spider the fly, the fly the frog
That was singing under the water:
When the man began to sing
Came his mother-in-law and made
   him shut up.

The verses continue through as many insects or animals that you choose until
the verses which contains all.

La Rana

Es - ta-ba-la ra-na can tan-do-de baj-o del

a - gua_____ cuan-do la a - ra - ña se puse a can-

tar vi - no la mos - ca y la hi - zo ca - llar ca-

lla-ba la mos-ca la rana que es-ta-ba can - tan-do de-ba-jo del

a - gua_____ cuan-do la mos - ca se pus - so a can-

tar vi - no la - a - ra na y la hizo callar_____

junio

JUNE

diás feriados
HOLIDAYS

junio (June) Contents

June English/Spanish Vocabulary

Bethlehem	Belén
bride	la novia
cakes	las tortas
coins	las monedas
crown	la corona
customs	las costumbres
dolls	las muñecas
firecrackers	los petardos
fireworks	los fuegos artificiales
groom	el novio
hay	el heno
husband	el esposo
journey	el viaje
night	la noche
shoes	los zapatos
stair	la escalera
toys	los juguetes
trick	la trampa (prank)
wedding	la boda
welcome	bienvenidos
wife	la esposa

El Día de los Reyes Magos
(The Day of the Three Kings)

El Día de los Reyes Magos, or the Day of the Three Kings, is celebrated every year in Mexico on January 6.

The three kings were named Melchior, Kaspar, and Balthasar. When Jesus was born, they came to Bethlehem to see the baby Jesus and arrived when he was twelve days old. They brought gifts. Children in Mexico believe the "magi" or wisemen bring them gifts on this day as well.

Mexican children leave their shoes on the outside step or balcony the night of January 5. They also remember to leave water and hay for the camels who have brought the kings on their journey. The next morning the hay and water have disappeared and the shoes are filled with small clay toys, candies and fruit. Special cakes, called "Roscas de Reyes," are baked in the shape of a crown. There are also usually little surprises baked inside, such as coins or little dolls. The lucky person who receives a gift inside the cake must prepare the party and cake for the following year.

Celebrated in Christian churches as the Epiphany, Mexican children may reenact the journey of the magi, usually with 3 boys depicting the kings.

Cuaresma Y Pascua
(Lent and Easter)

Cuaresma, Lent, begins with Ash Wednesday and Mexican families generally go to church to begin the 40 day period which ends on Pascuas or Easter. Cuaresma is characterized by special foods such as Torta de camarón, kind of shrimp omelet. Families also usually eat only one large meal a day with no meat on Friday. A popular Lenten dessert is "Capirotada," a sweet bread pudding.

Semana Santa, or the final week of Lent is the most eventful. The week begins on Sunday with the blessing of the palms. Each member of the family brings a palm, flower, or plant to the church to be blessed. Families appear like "walking gardens" as they make their way to church in their finest clothes. There may be processions during the week bearing statues of the Holy Family. On Thursday night the "arrest" of Jesus is enacted and, on Friday, the entire Passion Play. The "trial" usually begins in the morning around eleven followed by events all day. There is a "mass of Glory" on Saturday. The day may also include a procession in which a statue of Judas, made of paper maché or straw is paraded, then set on fire with strings of firecrackers, amid much shouting and noise. Sunday is a time of joy. There may be feasts and "cascarones," egg shells decorated and filled with confetti, which are thrown back and forth in fun.

Día de las Madres
(Mother's Day)

Mother's Day is celebrated on the 10th of May in Mexico. Mothers may be remembered with small gifts or flowers, as in the United States. It is also traditional to assemble a "gallo" or group of Musicians, to come to the house early in the morning and serenade the woman with favorites such as "Las Mañanitas." The singers may be members of the family, or they may be hired from a mariachi group or other musical band.

Día de Corpus Christi
(The Day of Corpus Christi)

Corpus Christi Day is usually celebrated in June, about the time of the summer solstice. People dress in white. Special honey sweets, flowers and tiny mules made of cornhusks are part of the celebration.

The Flying Pole Dance is performed on this day. Five men climb a tall pole, perhaps as tall as a 1000 feet. One man stays perched on the top of the pole beating a drum and playing a small flute. The others are "fliers" who wrap a rope around their waists, and as the drum beats, fly around the pole, unwinding from the rope. They must be able to make thirteen revolutions from the top to the bottom. This dangerous dance is believed to have originated as a tribute to the sun god in Veracruz.

Día de San Juan de Bautista
(The Day of John the Baptist)

The Day of John the Baptist, is usually celebrated on June 24. This day is remembered by symbolic and fun water play. Swimming parties are organized and it is customary to be sprinkled with water. Gently sprinkling one's friends, parents, or teachers is all part of the fun.

Día de los Santos Inocentes

December 28, El Día de los Santos Inocentes, is the equivalent of our April Fools Day. Little tricks are played on friends in the spirit of fun.

Inocente palomita
Que tú dejaste engañar
Sabiendo que en este día
¡Nada se debe prestar!

Innocent Little Dove
You have let yourself be fooled,
Knowing that on this day
You should lend nothing!

Blessing of the Animals

The blessing of the animals occurs on January 17, the day of Saint Anthony the Abbot. Family pets or barnyard animals are decorated with flowers, streamers, and even sometimes painted. They are then paraded to the church to be blessed by the priest.

Bautizo
(Baptism)

Christening is a big event in many Mexican families. It may be the first time the mother and child are seen in public since the birth. Padrinos, godparents, are chosen for the special task of following the child as it grows, giving support to the parents, and participating in the special events of the child's life.

Quinceañera
(Coming of Age)

One of the loveliest Mexican traditions is the Quinceañera, or "coming of age" celebration for young women. This custom is thought to have originated with the Aztecs, who believed a woman did not become a human being until she was fifteen. The ceremony is meant not only to welcome the girl into womanhood, but into the church as well. A special mass is arranged for the girl and is attended by family and friends. The dress, reception, and dance are similar to that found at a wedding.

Bodas
(Weddings)

The Mexican wedding or "boda" is a blend of traditional and modern customs. Many marriages are still arranged by the families of the couple with the help of an intermediary, although it is also common for young people to decide for themselves who they will marry.

Traditionally, the "petición de la mano" is asked by the groom's family after several visits to the family of the bride. The first visit is characterized by much general conversation before the subject of the marriage is approached. On each of these preliminary visits, the groom's father brings gifts to the house of the bride to show his sincerity and ability to provide. Three weeks before the wedding, the engaged couple is presented at the church and received by the priest. The day before the wedding, the couple is taken to church by the godparents for communion and confession. After the ceremony they are received at home with a small reception.

While the groom is responsible for the general expenses of the wedding, the "padrinos" or godparents help with certain parts of the wedding tradition. The "padrinos de narro" arrange for the bridal bouquet. The "padrinos de lazo" provide the bride's Bible, rosary, and the lazo (a silk cord wrapped around the couple during the ceremony to signify their union). The "padrinos de arras" provide the 13 pieces of silver money and the 3 wedding rings. The priest blesses the silver and the rings as he greets the couple at the entrance to the church. Two of the rings are placed on the brides hand and one on the groom's. The groom lets the silver slip into the hand of the bride, symbolizing the hope that his earnings will be plentiful and that he will share them with his bride. The silver is then left at the church at the close of the ceremony to be given to charity. Many church ceremonies include Mariachi bands or other special music.

After the mass has been given, the bride may leave her bouquet at the feet of the Virgin before she leaves the church. The ceremony is usually followed by feasting and dancing.

Las Mañanitas
(Happy Birthday Song)

Estas son las mañanitas que cantaba el Rey David
Hoy por ser día de tu santo, te las cantamos a tí.
Despierta, mi bien, despierta, mira que ya amaneció,
Ya los pajaritos cantan, la luna ya se metió.

Qué linda está la mañana en que vengo a saludarte,
Venimos todos con gusto y placer a felicitarte.
Ya viene amaneciendo, ya la luz del día nos dio,
Levántate de mañana, mira que ya amaneció.

Manuel M. Ponce (1949)
Luis Mars (1948)

arranged by Stanley A. Lucero

lin - da es ta la ma - ña - na

En que ven - go a sa - lu-

dar - te ___ ve - ni - mos

to - dos con gus - to ___ y pla-

cer a fe - li - ci - tar - te ___

ya vie - ne a - ma - ne -

cien - do ___ ya la luz del

día nos dío ___ Le - van-

ta - te de ma - ña - na ___ mi - ra

que ya a - ma - ne ció ___

julio

JULY

México
hoy en día

MEXICO TODAY
FAMOUS MEXICANS

julio (July) Contents

México – Hoy en Día
Mexico Today

Mexico is located to the south of the United States. It is a country of such contrasts that it is important to point them out. Many of these contrasts are probably evident after studying all the material that is included here in this book for each chapter is filled with the old and the new ways of Mexico.

Parts of Mexico are as streamlined and modern as the most contemporary times will allow and other parts have not changed since recorded time in Mexico. Let's look at a few.

It is possible for a person in the United States to step across into Mexico at any point along the 1500-mile border that runs from the Pacific Ocean to Brownsville, Texas. Yet, when you cross that border, life changes along with the customs. The country draws people from all over the world to shop for many treasures and products, to learn about Mexican culture and the people, to swim and fish in the beautiful oceans and to see the heritage that is so rich.

One thing that is so fascinating to the tourists is the mixture of old and new. For example, on the edge of modern Mexico City, there is an old temple called Cuicuilco which was built by unknown prehistoric peoples 8,500 years ago. You can swim and sun in gigantic, luxury hotels in Cancún and then take a short bus trip to the ruins of Chízen-Itza, the Maya pyramids. Also, on the same trip you can leave your spacious rooms only to pass grass huts that have not changed since the time of the Maya except to, perhaps, add an electric light bulb in the center of the hut. The women are out in back, washing their clothes in a tub while using a rock and sand to clean the clothes rather than the machine they are using in the city.

If you are close enough to a school, you might find room to go to school with over 50 children in a classroom in the very rural areas and yet, in Mexico City, there is the University City with 80 streamlined and colorful buildings. It has a stadium that seats 80,000 people, a cosmic ray laboratory, and the world's largest Olympic swimming pool.

Tourists are often surprised to see Aztec dancers on the streets in downtown Mexico City. The dances are very religious and it does not seem to bother the dancers that people are watching.

In many parts of Mexico there are modern industrial parts right next to a small "pueblo" where the people make handicrafts for a living. One of the joys of Mexico is that so many of their beautiful crafts and art works are handmade by these people. These objects made one at a time and hand-painted or handmade are basically the same as their ancestors made hundreds of years ago.

In the country, it is common to see people still guiding their burros in the native costumes with jet planes soaring overhead. The farmers still plant corn with a stick as did their Maya ancestors years ago.

In 1968, when the workmen began the excavation for the "Metro" (subway), they uncovered the ruins of the Aztec capital. The archeologists uncovered and the workmen followed and as you ride the subway today, you pass beautiful objects that they have left for your enjoyment. More than 500,000 objects of Aztec and Spanish history were uncovered.

In any large Mexican city these days, you can find the "supermercados," super markets, that are the same as the ones you have in your city; however, all the prices are in "pesos." *Note: the rate of the peso changes daily and the exchange can be found in the business section of your daily newspaper. Currently, it is anywhere from 2500 pesos to an American dollar on up. It is a good exercise for children who are learning to add and subtract in thousands.

Only a few blocks away, you might be able to find "mercados," markets, where the women carry their own bags and select their wares or food from different stalls and carry them home in their bag. This is similar to a flea market.

It is also common to find outdoor markets with the merchandise spread out on mats. A crude piece of canvas might be overhead to protect them from the sun. These movable markets are very much like the Aztec markets which one of Cortés' soldiers described more than four hundred years ago. The main difference is that change is given in "centavos," cents, instead of cocoa beans.

The landscape is also full of contrasts with snow-covered volcanoes and high mountain ranges to green valleys. There are rain forests filled with enchanting birds and animals and desert regions with snakes and cactus. Many of these are but a few miles apart.

Consider for a minute the center of Mexico city which is called the Zócalo. On this ground today stand the National Palace and Supreme Court, the municipal government building and the Metropolitan Cathedral — one of the oldest churches in the New World. Directly beneath these buildings lie the ruins of the city of Tenochitlán, the capital of the Aztecs. In some of the old buildings near the Zócalo can be found stones carved by Indians in the 14th and 15th centuries to walls erected by their conquerors in the 16th, 17th and 18th centuries.

Mexico is 75,000 square miles, about one-quarter the size of the United States. It is a Republic with twenty-nine states, two territories and a Federal district that is similar to that of Washington D.C.

At least two-thirds of Mexico is mountainous. They are high and rugged and the result of volcanoes. Although the mountains are beautiful, they separate the peoples and they have affected the history and development of the country greatly. The two highest mountain ranges are along each coast. They are called the Eastern Sierra Madre and the Western Sierra Madre. They run more than half the length of the country. Just below Mexico City they come together and then continue as only one range known as the Southern Sierra Madre.

Millions of years ago, many beautiful volcanic peaks were created two of which guard Mexico City and are known as Popcátepetl and Ixtaccihuatl. "Popo" is also called the Smoking Mountain and Ixtaccihuatl is affectionately called the "Sleeping Lady." There is a legend about the two volcanoes which is very similar to "Romeo and Juliet" which explains why the two are so close.

In February, 1943, there was a farmer and his family working in a field when there was a sudden earthquake and before Dionisio Pulido's eyes, appeared a fissure with sulfurous fumes, smoke and ashes pouring fourth. By evening the rising cloud of smoke could be seen in the village, Paricutín, and during the night, red-hot rocks were seen shooting into the air.

Within a week of its erupting, the cone had reached a peak of 500 feet. By April, the volcano caused the evacuation of the village and in June, another village nearby had to be abandoned.

By the end of the year, the volcano had grown to 900 feet. The eruptions continued until February 25, 1952, just 9 years and 4 days since it's birth. The rim of the crater then stood 1,345 feet above Dionisio Pulido's cornfield. Its lava had covered more than ten miles and had destroyed two villages. It was man's opportunity to witness and study a volcano from its beginning to its end.

There are not many rivers in Mexico. Many of them are underground. Lakes, too, are scarce. Two lakes are Lake Chapala in the state of Jalisco and Lake Pátzcuaro in the state of Michoacán. Tarascan Indians still fish today in dugout canoes with butterfly nets as did their ancestors.

The Central Plateau has two basic seasons: rainy and dry. The rainy season is from May to October and the dry season is from November to May.

Temperatures on the seacoasts average 70 degrees in the winter to 100 degrees in the summer which explains why Mexico's coastal cities are such a popular place to visit.

FAMOUS

MEXICANS

Benito Juárez

Benito Juárez was one of Mexico's greatest political leaders. Known for his honesty and concern for the poor, he is often called the "Abraham Lincoln" of Mexico.

Juárez was a Zapotec Indian who was born in the state of Oaxaca. He practiced law there and became active in politics in the 1840's. Juárez joined the "liberal" forces and became governor of Oaxaca in 1847. The liberals sought a constitutional government, redistribution of land, and the abolition of church abuses for all of Mexico. Juárez was exiled in 1853 but was able to return in 1855.

He became provisional president during the "War of Reform," 1858-60. He was elected president in 1861. He sought to stabilize the government's serious financial debts by suspending foreign interest payments, and incurred the wrath of France. French troops invaded Mexico and Maximillian was installed as emperor. Juárez fled, but was able to return again after Maximillian was executed in 1867.

Juárez again became president and instituted such reforms as: separation of church and state, redistribution of land, and religious tolerance. He even sought public education for women who, previously did not have access to public schooling. Juárez is remembered more than anything for his commitment to civil liberties for all Mexicans.

José Guadalupe Posada
(1852-1913)

José Guadalupe Posada was a Mexican artist, famous for his paintings of *calaveras*, or skulls. This is the name used for the traditional poems written to celebrate the Day of the Dead.

Posada worked as a teacher and an engraver before he was able to work as an artist for the Mexico City publisher, Venegas Arroyos. Posada and Arroyos used their talents to work for reforms and to expose corrupt politicians of the day.

It is the custom for newspapers in Mexico to publish political cartoons and poems during the celebration of the "Day of the Dead." Posada is now recognized as a great artist, even though during his lifetime his talent was relatively unrecognized. His work was an inspiration to two other great modern Mexican artists; Diego Rivera and José Clemente Orozco, who also found their subjects within the Indian-Spanish culture.

César Chávez

César Chávez was born near Yuma, Arizona in 1927. Born into a family of migrant workers, he learned at an early age about "life in the fields." He was able to attend school through the sixth grade but left to go to work. He spent his teenage years working with his family in fields throughout the southwest.

César served in the Navy during World War II. He married in 1948 and went to work for the Community Service Organization. It was at CSO that César met Dolores Huerta who would become his assistant in later years. He was successful at CSO, helping to organize local chapters and coordinate leadership in the west. He stayed there until 1962, when he left to devote himself full-time to organizing farm workers.

In 1966, he was able to establish the first farm workers' union, the National Farm Workers' Association. In 1968, Chávez urged the nation to recognize the needs of farm laborers with the boycott of California table grapes. His non-violent strategies and his personal commitment and charisma gained him the national attention he needed. In 1970, 26 growers signed contracts with Chávez guaranteeing higher wages, and other needed reforms.

Today, Chávez continues as a leader in the struggle for fair labor contracts and working conditions for farm workers.

José Clemente Orozco

José Clemente Orozco is one of Mexico's greatest painters. He was born in 1883 in the state of Jalisco. As a young man, he worked to revive the art of fresco painting as part of the government sponsored group, the Syndicate of Painters and Sculptors. His frescos of the Revolutionary period are among the most famous for their exquisite depiction of the Mexican workers.

Orozco came to the United States in 1927 and painted frescos in a number of U.S. colleges. During the 1930's, he returned to Mexico and painted some of his greatest murals in Mexico City and Guadalajara. During his later years he experimented with medium and style but retained the theme so evident in all of his work; the struggle of humanity.

David Alfaro Siqueiros

A contemporary of Orozco, Siqueiros stands out as another of the great Mexican painters. He was born in Chihuahua in 1886 and from the time he was a young man maintained an interest in both painting and revolutionary politics. He went to school until he was 17, then joined the revolutionary forces of Carranza. When he was 23, he went to Europe to study art and to travel. He returned three years later to assume leadership for the Mexican government, as part of the Painter's syndicate. He, along with Orozco and others, executed murals at many schools and government buildings in Mexico during this period.

During this time Siquieros became heavily involved in politics and began helping to organize unions and publish pro-labor literature. He continued to paint both in Mexico and the United States until 1936, when he went to Spain to participate in the Spanish Civil War. On his return to Mexico, he continued his political activities until his later years. His murals and other paintings continued to reflect the revolutionary theme and revolutionary techniques until his death in Cuernavaca in 1974.

Diego Rivera

Diego Rivera is another one of the Mexican "masters." He was born in 1886 in Guanajuato. Like Siquieros, he attended art classes at a young age, then went to Europe to study art in Spain, France, and Italy. When he returned to Mexico in 1921, he was also a leader in the government sponsored Painter's Syndicate. He developed his own techniques for painting large mural surfaces and was in great demand to paint both in Mexico and the United States.

During the 1930's, he changed from mural painting and concentrated on easel work of portraits or landscapes of Mexican life. In the 1940's he returned once again to murals. Like his contemporaries Orozco and Siquieros, his paintings often invoke religious or political controversy. Rivera died in 1957 in Mexico City.

Octavio Paz

Octavio Paz is one of Mexico's leading writers. He was born in 1914 in Mexico City. He incorporates Aztec, Marxist, Oriental and surrealistic ideas into his writing. His unique style and his writings on many subjects make his work widely read in Mexico.

"The Labyrinth of Solitude" is one of his most popular works. It is a collection of essays which reflect the lives and character of the Mexican people.

Today, Paz lives in Mexico City still writing his thoughts about life and his people.

Luisa Moreno

Although not Mexican born, Luisa Moreno played an important role in organizing Mexican workers in the United States. She married a Mexican and lived there until she immigrated to New York in 1928. In Mexico City she had worked as a newspaper correspondent and poet. In New York she obtained a job in one of the garment factories. Conditions were deplorable.

In 1933, she helped organize labor strikes in Harlem for a union which later merged with the International Ladies Garment Worker's Union. In 1935 she joined the American Federation of Labor as an organizer. Later she helped to form the CIO. Luisa was convinced that the progress of unions for Spanish speaking workers depended on progress in the protection of civil rights.

Luisa organized the first Congress of Spanish Speaking People in Los Angeles in 1939. The congress focused on the needs of Spanish speaking people in the areas of health, work, and education. It gained national attention and led to a congressional investigation into the protection of civil rights for Mexican workers.

Chicanos

(The History of the Mexican People in California)

There are many Hispanics in the United States today from all over the world. In Florida there is a large population of Cubans, in New York there are the Puertoicans and throughout the United States are people from South and Central America. Special attention is being placed here on the Chicanos for they are the people of Mexico.

An interesting phenomena is that, in the city of Los Angeles, the population of Spanish speaking people has almost made a complete turn around in history. Before California was a state, the people living in the area were from Mexico. At the time of the gold rush, thousands of people flooded California to look for gold and, being residents, they knew how to acquire the land and soon the Mexicans lost their property and were sent back to Mexico. The white was the dominant race; however, very soon in the future, the Spanish-speaking residents will out number the whites.

The history of the Chicanos can be traced to the missionaries, soldiers, and civilian colonists and their struggle to maintain their identity. They are a diverse group of people who have the common thread of a rich and colorful heritage. Many terms are used to describe them such as Latino, Latin American, Mexican American, Spanish speaking, Mexican, Raza, Chicano, Hispanic and others.

The movement of Mexicans north began nearly four hundred years ago with the first colonial settlement in Santa Fe, New Mexico in 1610. The surrounding lands began to attract more settlers mainly to get away from the Revolución in México and to discover new lands.

The missions had their effect on the colonizing of California with the first being established in San Diego in 1769. There were two other institutions in early California; the presidio which offered protection to the mission and the pueblo or town. The two first pueblos established were Los Angles and San Jose. The most characteristic of Alta California society during the colonial period was the life in an isolated area away from the cultural center of New Spain.

The news of Mexico's independence from Spain in 1821 was of little importance to Alta Californians under the governorship of the Spanish-born Pablo Vicente de Sola.

A major change occurred when the missions were secularized and the governor, José Figueroa in 1834 called for a systematic distribution of half of the mission's land to the Indians. The other half was administered by the secular agents to maintain the land for grazing livestock. Under this agreement, the Indians could not sell their land. The early death of Figuero opened the door to many abuses. Nevertheless, local towns were governed by "ayuntamientos" (town councils) and each province had a legislature of elected officials called "diputaciones."

The changes that a new form of government brought in California were seen in the social and class differences. The elite were a small group of mestizos — which were between 5 to 10 percent of the population. Most settlers lived in the pueblos of Los Angeles, San Diego, Santa Barbara, Monterey, Santa Cruz and San Jose. Nearly all men worked in such trades as "vaqueros" (cowboys), saddle-makers, silversmiths and blacksmiths. They lived in "adobe" homes and grazed their livestock on "ejidos" (public land). The "pobladores" (residents) also worked on a seasonal basis during the "rodeos" and "matanzas" (slaughters and round-ups) on the ranchos. Some congregated in small villages or "Rancherias."

Women worked along side the men in the fields and tended the livestock. Also, women were commonly the "curanderas" or folk healers.

Families worked together and few ever lacked food or shelter for they had the god-parent relationships — "compadrazgo" with "padrinos" and "madrinas" (god-fathers and god-mothers) taking their roles seriously.

An interest in California grew in the 1840's partially due to its exceptional coast but also due to President James K. Polk's desire to expand and to acquire the northern lands of Mexico. John C. Fremont and his Bear Flag Revolt to create an independent republic in California was short-lived as it immediately went into the hands of the United States.

In 1848 with the signing of the Treaty of Guadalupe, California was annexed to the United States. However, by 1850, gold had been discovered and the Mexican state of California quickly became "American."

Practically overnight the demographic profile of the state changed. Not only was California inundated with Anglo-Americans but there were also Chinese and other foreigners. Although the Treaty of Guadalupe Hidalgo guaranteed "the enjoyment of all the rights in the United States. . ." it did not specify the property claims and, as a result, the Mexicans lost their land.

During the 1850's and into the 1860's, racial tensions grew. To the Mexicans, "foreigners" were creating a new society which held little respect for the earliest residents and their traditions. To the Americans, "backward Mexicans" were impeding progress and Americanization.

The "rancho" cattle came into a slump in the late 1850's after the gold-rush and with the importation of beef cattle from other states, the Ranchos began to break up and the land was sold to the Anglos. Economic poverty and unemployment became the way of life for the Mexican whereas, it gave the Anglos an opportunity to gain controls.

Mexicans, in the face of increasing social and residential segregation, tried to maintain their former life styles by staying together in the "barrios" (neighborhoods). This insured the continuity of the religious practices, the Spanish language, culture, customs and, most of all, the closeness of the family ties. Social political and cultural clubs were formed to celebrate traditional holidays and fiestas.

Prior to the 1920's, Mexicans could come and go across the border with little difficulty. They were "cheap" labor and were used in agriculture and in railroading. The Mexican Revolution also brought many Mexicans to California to escape the regime of Porfírio Díaz. It is said that between 1910 and 1930 that nearly a tenth of Mexico's population fled to the United States.

As the number of Mexican residents increased, so did the awareness of the public. The "barrios" were filled with people and children and the recognition that the Mexicans were not just visitors, but were here to stay finally hit the general public.

The stock-market crash of 1929 was particularly hard on the poor and ethnic minorities. The feeling developed that the Mexicans were taking jobs away from others, they were on welfare rolls and that the Mexicans were not here legally and should not be part of the welfare system. Over 75,000 Mexicans were deported to Mexico between 1931 and 1933. It did not matter if they were legal or not.

Nothing has done more to symbolize the hostility towards the Chicano in the 1930's and 1940's than the Sleepy Lagoon Case and the Zoot Suit Riots. Both took place in Los Angeles, California.

The media had centered on the youth or the "pachuco" which were members of local clubs or neighborhood gangs of both girls and boys. They dressed in a distinctive manner with high pompadoured ducktail haircuts, tattoos, and baggy zoot-suits for the boys and short skirts, bobby sox and heavy make-up for the girls. They were easily identified by the language they spoke called "caló" a mixture of English and Spanish. They were a mixture of youth who did not see themselves as either Mexican or American.

Sleepy Lagoon was a swimming hole where the gangs would "hang out." The body of a young Chicano was found and the police arrested, and the Grand Jury indicted, 22 members of the 38th Street Club for murder. In 1944, state senator Jack Tenney and his committee succeeded in persuading the District Court of Appeal to reverse the decision and the defendants were released from San Quentin prison.

The Zoot Suit Riots of 1943 were even more discriminatory. On June 3, 1943, rumors were circulated that Chicanos had beaten sailors involving some young Mexican women. The newspaper picked up on the rumor and soon sailors and soldiers from bases nearby, converged on the streets downtown and beat every Mexican, zoot-suit or not, while the police watched from the sidelines.

Many Mexicans served valiantly in World War I with a voluntary enlistment larger than any other ethnic group. Even more served in World War II, Korea and Viet Nam. Seventeen Mexicanos received the Congressional Medal of Honor and Company E, 141st Regiment of the 36th (Texas) Division was the most highly decorated of all the groups and was comprised of Mexicans.

In World War II, those in the 101st "Screaming Eagles," were among the first advance force that parachuted behind German lines at the beginning of the Normandy landings – the first Americans to do battle on French land. They were the Mexican-American paratroopers.

During World War II, most young men of all ethnic groups joined the armed forces. This created a need for workers in the fields. During this time, many Mexicans were allowed to enter the United States as farm laborers called "braceros." As many as 120,000 braceros were admitted in 1945 and the program continued until 1964.

The creativity of the Chicanos came to the eyes of the public with murals in Los Angeles and San Diego, the Teatro Campesino and the plays directed by Luis Valdez (most known for *Zoot Suit*), political posters by Rupert García and Malaqüis Montoya and many published works of prose and poetry.

The main contribution of the Chicano movement has been in the positive self-identity that it has fostered in the Americans from Mexico.

The Legend of
Joaquin Murieta and Tiburcio Vázquez

The legend of Joaquin Murieta is one of the most famous of Mexican American "bandidos" (bandits).

Murieta came from Sonora during the gold rush and became involved with the "gringos" in response to their treatment of the Mexicans.

Legend has it that the miners killed his wife, hung his brother and beat him to steal his mine. He became a shrewd highwayman and robbed and killed to avenge the treatment he had received. Sightings of Murieta were seen up and down the California coast in the 1850's.

Murieta was a hero in the eyes of the Mexicans for he stood as a symbol of one who would not submit to the Anglo authority in California and for that he was named "The Robin Hood of El Dorado."

Tiburcio Vázquez, the last of the "bandidos," also was a symbol of resistance to the Anglos. Vázquez was a native of California, born in Monterrey. He, too, had several run-ins with the law and began a life of crime and revenge.

He was sent to San Quentin prison and when he was released the police started to bother him again. His response was to return to crime in robbing the Americans of cattle and cash.

His most famous exploit was in the 1870's when he became famous for his daring robberies in northern California. He was chased by a posse for 2,000 miles. The posse finally found him in a ranch house outside of Los Angeles in an area now called Vázquez Rocks. Tiburcio was wounded, arrested and taken to San Jose where he was tried and sentenced to be hanged. Before his execution, he explained to a newspaper reporter why he had turned to a life of crime.

"My career grew out of the circumstances by which I was surrounded. As I grew to manhood I was in the habit of attending balls and parties given by the native Californians, into which the Americans, then beginning to become numerous, would force themselves and shove the native-born men aside, monopolizing the dance and the women. This was about 1852. A spirit of hate and revenge took possession of me. I had numerous fights in defense of my countrymen. The officers were continually in pursuit of me. I believed we were unjustly and wrongfully deprived of the social rights that belonged to us."

Mexico – Country of Contrasts

Materials:
cigar box with the lid attached, construction paper, grass seed, crayons or markers, dirt.

1. Cut the paper to fit inside the lid of the cigar box.

2. Draw a background scene of volcanos behind Mexico City (or pyramids).

3. Fill the cigar box with dirt. Add twigs (trees) buildings, rocks etc.

4. Sprinkle grass in any bare area and watch it grow!

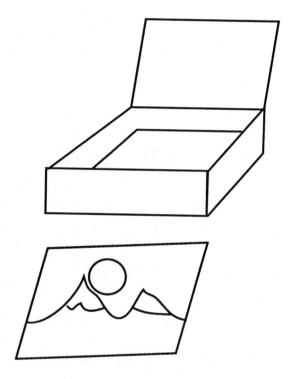

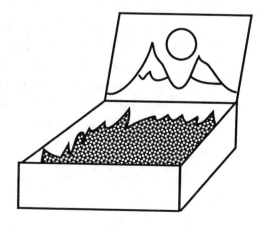

Vocabulary

ballpoint pen	el bolígrafo
book	el libro
ceiling	el techo
chair	la silla
chalk	la tiza
chalkboard	la pizarra
desk (teacher's)	el escritorio
desk (student's)	el pupitre
door	la puerta
eraser	el borrador
floor	el piso
friend	el amigo (boy), la amiga (girl)
grades	las calificaciones
homework	la tarea
paper	el papel
paper clip	el sujetapapeles
pen	la pluma
pencil	el lápiz
pencil sharpener	el sacapunto
principal	el director (man), la directora (woman)
projector (movie)	el proyector
record	el disco
record player	el tocadiscos
ruler	la regla
scotch tape	cinta adhesiva
slide projector	el proyector de diapositivas
stapler	la grapadora
staples	las grapas
tape	la cinta
tape recorder	la grabadora
teacher	el maestro (man), la maestra (woman)
trash	la basura
textbook	el texto, el libro de texto
window	la ventana

Reference Books

Camarillo, Albert, *Chicanos in California*, Boyd and Fraser Publishing Co., California

Copeland, John G., Ralph Kite and Lynn Sandstedt, *Literatura y Arte*, Holt, Rinehart & Winston, 1985.

"Copy Cat Publications," Volume 3, Copycat Press, Inc. WI 1990.

Coronado, Rosa, *Cooking the Mexican Way*, Lerner Pub. Minneapolis, 1982.

de Pala, Tomie, *Nuestra Senora de Guadalupe*, Holiday House, New York, 1980.

Earth Works Group, The, *30 Simple Things Kids Can Do To Save the Earth*, The Earth Works Group, MI.

Fawcett, Raymond, *How Did They Live?*, Robert Bentley, Inc., 1954.

Funk and WAgnalls, New Encyclopedia, Dun & Bradstreet, USA, Vol. 17.

Gabet, Marcia, *Fun With Social Studies*, Teacher Created Materials, CA.

Garcia, Joe Dell & Mabel Otis Robison, *Come Along to Mexico*, T.S. Denison, MN, 1971.

Griego, Margot C., *Tortillas Para Mama*, Henry Holt and Co., NY.

Herring, Hubert, *A History of Latin America*, Alfred A. Knopf, New York, 1969.

IDEA Inc., *Provoking Thoughts*, "Mayan Math," IDEA, Inc., MN 1989.

"La Raza Cultural Series," The National Hispanic University, Oakland CA,

Los Amiguitos, *Cancionero Infantil*, Ass'n. of Mexican American Education, CA 1983.

Lucero, Stanley, *Canciones Para Niños*, Ass'n. of Mexican American Education, 1983.

May, Rosalind G, *Exciting Things to Make With Wool, String and Thread*, J.B. Lippincott Co., 1977.

May, Stella Burke, *My Neighbor Mexico*, The Fidler Co., Michigan 1941.

"México Visto Por Sus Ninos," The Latin America Project/SPICE, Stanford Univ., 1983 pg. 12.

National Geographic Magazine October 1984 Vol. 166 #4, "Following the Route of Cortes"

National Geographic Magazine, October. 1989 Vol. 176, #4 "La Ruta Maya."

National Geographic Magazine, April 1986 Vol. 169 #4 "Río Azul: Lost City of the Maya"

National Geographic Magazine, Dec. 1975 Vol. 148 #6, "The Maya: Children of Time."

National Geographic Magazine, August 1981 Vol. 160 #2, "Maya Art Discovered in Cave."

National Hispanic University, CA 94606.

Oakland Unified School District, *Resource Guide for Bi-lingual Children*, Oakland Unified School District, CA.

Perl, Lila, *Piñatas and Paper Flowers,* Clarion Books, New York, 1983.

Rascon, Vincent, *A Mexican-American Coloring Book*, Polaris Press, CA 95303

Reader's Digest, *Natural Wonders of the World*, Reader's Digest, NY 1980.

Salinas-Norman, Bobbi, *Folk Art Traditions*, Piñata Publications, Oakland, CA 1987 Vol. I, II.

Stein, R. Conrad, *Enchantment of the World, Mexico*, Children's Press, Chicago, 1984.

Schubert, Barbara and Marlene Bird, *Mexican*, Reflections and Images, CA 1976.

Singer, Jane and Kurt, *Folktales of Mexico*, T.S. Denison, MN.

Taylor, Frank, Alfred Artuso & Frank Hewett, *Creative Art Tasks For Children*, Love Publishing Co., Colorado 1970.

Tooer, Frances, *Mexican Popular Arts*, Blaine Ethridge Books, Detroit, 1973.

Tooer, Frances, *Treasury of Mexican Folkways*, Crown Pub. Co., NY 1947.

West, John O., *Mexican-American Folklore*, August House Pub., Ark., 1988.

Witton, Dorothy, *Our World Mexico*, Simon and Schuster, NY.

Woman's Day, *Encyclopedia of Cookery*, Fawcett-Haynes, Maryland, 1966, Vol. VII.

World Book, Inc., *The World Book Encyclopedia*, USA, 1984, Vol. 11.